Praise

Jim Smith has done it again. He has picked up the approach from his first book and pushed it right to the core of the current educational buzz word: 'progress'.

'Progress' has become one of those words which it is easy to say, but harder to treat with respect. Hence it risks being treated with lip service by pupils, by teachers and at whole school level as people look over their shoulders at those who are watching them. This book cuts through all that, and offers a wealth of ideas for treating the word 'progress' seriously and ensuring that pupils have a chance of making some and knowing they have.

Using the techniques of his first book, Jim offers idea upon idea in a way that is entirely accessible. The Lazy bit is again a misnomer but the book does show how thinking teachers and school leaders can make their jobs enjoyable and reap the rewards for effort that makes sense.

Mick Waters, Professor of Education,
Wolverhampton University

A welcome sequel to Jim Smith's first book, and again jam-packed with ideas for invisibly transferring the learning load onto students – this time with an emphasis on whole-school processes. Readable, amusing and quirky, I expect this to do as well as its predecessor.

Barry J. Hymer, Professor of Psychology in Education,
Education Faculty, University of Cumbria

Following the success of his first book, *The Lazy Teacher's Handbook*, Jim Smith continues his exploration of ways in which everyone involved in schools, from NQTs to senior leaders, is responsible for ensuring that learning and progress are at the heart of the business of teaching, the Lazy Way.

Of interest to any practising teacher, the thorny issue of lesson observations is unpacked and the process of demonstrating 'outstanding' teaching demystified. He looks in particular at what is meant by 'progress' and how this can be planned for, and then demonstrated, within a lesson observation. Importantly, however, he doesn't lose sight of the fact that teaching is a highly interpersonal activity carrying many rewards beyond a successful Ofsted grade.

When looking at professional development for teachers, the Lazy Way – encouraging teachers to take responsibility for their own development – is proposed and new approaches to CPD and performance management are suggested. At the heart of this lies the belief that teachers are highly skilled professionals with the potential to innovate, provided they are given the opportunity.

Still a practising teacher himself, Jim Smith writes with authority and also with respect for both the young people that he teaches and the colleagues with whom he works. Underpinned by a clearly articulated paradigm and written in a refreshing, engaging and accessible style, punctuated with examples drawn from his own work and from his extensive experience of working with a range of schools, this book speaks to anyone who is (or will be) part of a busy staffroom and who seeks more than a set of tips for teachers.

Jayne Prior, Senior Teaching Fellow in Education and Director of Educational and Professional Studies (PGCE), University of Bristol

Being a self-confessed fan of the Lazy Way and having read *The Lazy Teacher's Handbook*, seen Jim Smith deliver INSET and been fortunate to visit the home of Lazy Teaching in Clevedon, I greeted this book with a measure of excitement and a dose of Ofsted weary cynicism. Excitement at the idea of more offbeat, yet enormously effective, strategies for delivering effective progress in my classroom; and cynicism at the potential for the approach to have taken on the age old appearance of simply being last year's educational fad.

Fortunately, I am writing this with yet more excitement and not a trace of cynicism. The book and its author maintain a sense of infectious enthusiasm, wonderful humour and genuinely intelligent comment on the educational landscape in 2012, allied to a rock solid approach to dealing with the challenging concept of ensuring every child makes progress in every lesson they encounter.

It is written in an easy, flowing style which allows you to take ideas on board and see how they relate to both current Ofsted requirements and contemporary educational thinking in general. It contains a constant stream of useful tips and strategies which can be adopted wholesale or picked carefully and adapted to your, and your class's, own style.

The lesson model provides real scope for development in your own school, whilst maintaining its theme of children developing the capacity to understand the concept of checking their own progress. Whilst the book attempts to be light-hearted and humorous, it addresses very real and very complex issues. It does this without being flippant or patronising and constantly recognises that teaching should be a job which teachers should thoroughly enjoy!

The book covers the use of data, effective lesson observation and the development of a whole school Lazy ethos. All are brought into the overall approach in a simple, sharp and rational manner which seems to make perfect sense. The seemingly endless, practical strategies which litter the text add to the feeling that you are reading a genuinely relevant and useful manual for teaching today.

The book is a thoroughly enjoyable, suitably humorous and endlessly useful read. It is a natural step from *The Lazy Teacher's Handbook* and takes the concept of Lazy Teaching out of the classroom and into the whole school.

Congratulations on another inevitable success, Jim.

Mind you ... I'm sure he's nicked a couple of my ideas!

Geoff Cherrill, Vice Principal, Nova Hreod, Swindon

FOLLOW ME, I'M RIGHT BEHIND YOU

Whole School Progress
the <u>LAZY</u> Way

Jim Smith

Edited by Ian Gilbert

 Independent Thinking Press

First published by

Independent Thinking Press
Crown Buildings, Bancyfelin, Carmarthen, Wales, SA33 5ND, UK
www.independentthinkingpress.com

Independent Thinking Press is an imprint of
Crown House Publishing Ltd.

British Library Cataloguing-in-Publication Data
A catalogue entry for this book is available
from the British Library.

Print ISBN 978-1-78135-006-5
Mobi ISBN 978-1-78135-018-8
ePub ISBN 978-1-78135-019-5

Printed and bound in the UK by
Bell & Bain Ltd, Glasgow

To Wendy, Henry and Oscar

Contents

Acknowledgements   iii

Foreword   v

Progress the Lazy Way – a Preface   ix

Introduction   1

1. Progress and the Lazy Inspector   5

2. Creating Progress in Your Lessons – The Lazy Way   19

3. Capturing Progress – The Lazy Way   57

4. Lazy Observations of Learning   87

5. Institutionalising Progress – In a Lazy Way   107

Progress the Lazy Way – an Epilogue   134

Recommended On-line Resources   137

Bibliography   137

Acknowledgements

This book would have still been so many ideas on bits of paper had it not been for the success of the first book. Hence, it seems appropriate to start by saying 'thank you' to all those who have grasped the idea of being 'lazy' and in one case demanded another book. I hope you like it, Mum!

It takes a team of people to turn lots of educational ideas on scraps of paper into a book, especially when some of the team may accuse me of following my Lazy Way when it comes to publishing as well as teaching! Therefore I want to acknowledge the work of Ian Gilbert who, in between sending pictures of some new amazing Chilean landscape, also finds time to guide, inspire and edit my thinking. Likewise, Caroline Lenton and the team at Independent Thinking Press. Caroline has offered unwavering support and encouragement (although without the amazing pictures).

Whether it is my 'day job' based in school or when I go out and about delivering the many INSET and Conference sessions I do, I am lucky to have different roles that continually provide me with the stimulus for ideas that are grounded in educational reality. So a huge thank you to my colleagues, delegates and of course the students, without whom we would never know if the ideas actually make a difference. Individual mention must go to Jamie Potter (Just Do It Wrong), David Didau (Learning Hexagons) and Gareth Beynon (Data Starts A Conversation) for offering ideas that really made me rush and write them down instantly.

As ever with a team it is those behind the scenes who play some of the most crucial roles. And in the case of Team Lazy it is no different. I owe a huge debt of gratitude to my gorgeous wife Wendy for her love, support and her regular doses of realism, which keep me grounded at all times (an excuse I often used during my off-days in the rugby lineout). Likewise our two boys, Henry and Oscar, for constantly reminding me what the most important thing in life is, as well as showing me just how amazing and quick learning can be – even if it does mean regularly coming third when we play games these days. To all three of you, not only a massive thank you, but an even bigger 'I love you' as well.

And finally, a huge thank you to everyone working in education. It makes a tremendous difference to millions of people. And by role modelling saying thank you, maybe it might just catch on. All the way to the top. You never know ...

Foreword

In his classic 1967 book, *The Medium is the Massage,** technology-in-society visionary Marshall McLuhan made a number of telling predictions about the nature of our modern world in the light of the technological revolution taking place at that time.

The changes – and remember, McLuhan was writing at a time when computers were THAT big – meant that people were beginning to shift from being passive observers of a simple world to becoming active participants in a complex, interconnected one. Further still, they were even players in the sort of game-changing scenario not seen since the invention of the printing press in which they were, as near as dammit, fusing with the world around them. As he famously wrote, 'The wheel is an extension of the foot; the book is an extension of the eye; clothing, an extension of the skin; electric circuitry, an extension of the central nervous system'.

Now, the fact that McLuhan's later work was entirely bonkers, something that was eventually found out to be the result of a brain tumour, should not detract from the fact that his predictions were of enormous significance, and whose value is only just becoming apparent. Way before a world in which Twitter, Facebook and other social media flourish, McLuhan was describing a world in which Twitter, Facebook and other social media *could* flourish. For education, his prophecy was of a significant battle between the old model and the new, a shift from teaching as direct instruction towards 'discovery – to probing and exploration and to the recognition of the language of forms'.

In a nutshell, a move from 'package to discovery'.

In this brave new educational world, McLuhan envisaged a classroom in which the learners were significantly more active in the

---

* Yes, 'massage', you heard right. It was a misprint, but when McLuhan saw it he deemed it rather apt and chose to keep it.

pursuit of their own knowledge than ever before, thanks in no small way to the freedom the new technologies gave them.

'As the audience becomes a participant in the total electric drama, the classroom can become a scene in which the audience performs an enormous amount of work.'

However, McLuhan's prophecies overlooked the fact that the biggest obstacle to this exciting world of whole-scale independent learning wasn't the technology. It was the teachers. But then again, he also failed to predict Angry Birds and Celebrity Big Brother.

Nor did he take into account Jim Smith and teaching done the Lazy Way.

Lazy Teaching is not about the use of technology to do away with the twenty-first century teacher. It's not about sitting students in front of rows of computer screens day after day. It's not even actually about being lazy. And it's certainly not a rejection of professionalism in the teaching workforce. Quite the opposite. Lazy Teaching came about through our observations in the classroom that if the teacher just got out of the way of the learning a little more often, everyone would benefit. And benefit significantly. After all, sometimes the best thing we can do to help young people learn is to stop teaching them. How can you expect anyone to learn anything *for themselves* when there's all that teaching going on?

Jim's first book, *The Lazy Teacher's Handbook*, was a tremendous success, not without its controversies of course, but it has become the bible for all those teachers who felt that 'working harder' wasn't the answer, despite the best exhortations of governments, inspectors and the management team. If you're banging your head against a brick wall, doing it harder is rarely the answer. By stepping back from all that teaching and letting children do so much more than they were doing before, you create a scenario in which everyone wins. In the words of one grateful acolyte writing to Jim recently:

I made the decision a couple of years ago to stop working harder than my students as I was feeling constantly disappointed and let down by them. I was doing so much and getting nothing in return.

I've since been feeling guilty as our system of management here is always blaming us for failing results and trying to get us to do more, monitor more, put on extra classes etc. However, in your book, I've found a like-minded individual; you've restored my faith in myself and my approach.

My grades are good and getting better and the kids love me!

Just one satisfied lazy customer amongst so many. What's more, on top of the pedagogical advantages to the approach, the stress-relieving benefits of the Lazy Way should not be under-estimated either. As one teacher wrote to Jim:

I'd just like to share a rather strange irony. I read your book in early June and announced to my boss that I planned to do 'no teaching' this coming year and that the learners would do all the work. She found it a bit difficult to swallow. In the middle of June I had a heart attack, and now I'm starting back this term with every intention of keeping my promise. I've everything prepared ready to be the really best lazy teacher, along with testimonials from my last cohort who love my lazy teaching methods, many of which of course are your methods.

Let's make it clear, your job shouldn't be a matter of life and death, it's not football, but with testimonials like that you realise that there is so much to be said for the Lazy Way. I am delighted, therefore, to be writing the foreword to Jim's new book in which he takes Lazy Teaching further, faster and lazier than ever before, applying it not only outside of the classroom and into the day-to-day to life of the school as a whole but also with a special focus on the inspector's current buzzword, 'progress'.

Now, 'progress might have been alright once, but it has gone on too long', as Ogden Nash once said, but learning without progress is rarely learning. I have seen too many lessons where children merely replicate what they have learnt and already know, giving the impression of a very bright class of knowledgeable souls yet who are actually missing out on the opportunity to be stretched further with every minute that ticks inexorably by. A focus on progress, however, says, 'I commit, as your teacher, to ensure you spend some of this lesson more stupid than you thought you were, and that you leave this classroom cleverer than when you entered it.'

And, when you combine this commitment to seeing your learners actually learning new things *each and every lesson* with a firm belief in the Lazy Way, then you have the opportunity for some really exciting, engaging, creative and wonderfully enjoyable lessons. With you working less in the process. Then throw in a whole-school approach to being Lazy that takes into account not just your lessons but also aspects of school life such as staff meetings, leadership and CPD and you have something quite special.

Enjoy, then, this second round of teaching done the Lazy Way from a master in the art of getting 'them' to do the work. In doing so you will not only help McLuhan's prophecies come true but also help yourself, your career and your health. As the teacher who wrote about doing so much and getting nowhere in return concluded in her missive to Jim:

Thanks so much. I really love my job and don't feel stressed or harassed one bit. In fact, I love getting up in the morning to go to work.

Lazy teachers who love getting up to go to work? Now there's a paradox, but as the great physicist Niels Bohr once said:

'How wonderful that we have met with a paradox. Now we have some hope of making progress.'

Ian Gilbert
May 2012

Progress the Lazy Way – a Preface

A few years ago I was asked by Independent Thinking to put together my thoughts and ideas for a book about what we called 'Lazy Teaching'. This was because (a) they wanted to get across the idea that, sometimes, the best thing we can do to help young people learn is to stop teaching them, in the traditional sense of the word, and (b) being a great big, 'outstanding' (not once but, ahem, twice inspected and thus acclaimed) Lazy Teacher myself I was the perfect person for the job.

The Lazy Teacher's Handbook became one of the biggest selling educational books of the last few years. This is something that has, ironically, led me to be working harder than ever, not only continuing my work in the senior leadership team and geography department of a secondary school wedged between the M5 and the Bristol Channel (and recently classed as 'outstanding' itself) but also working around the country helping other teachers adopt and adapt their own Lazy Teaching practices.

Of course, a book with such a title is not without its controversies, most notably the claim that being lazy is the antithesis of being a good professional teacher (more of 'Irate of Bucks' later). But teaching in the 'Lazy Way', as we came to call it, is quite the opposite of that – if you can have an antithesis of an antithesis without the universe imploding. The teacher's job is to engage their pupils and students in the best quality learning possible, for as long as possible and as often as possible. Learning is a personal, active process. The teacher at the front teaching is, for the learner, rarely personal and never active.

The Lazy Way, therefore, says that the more we can get the learner actively engaged in the pursuit, capture, employment and assessment of their own learning, the better. Which means planning lessons that are based around the learner learning and not the teacher teaching.

The Lazy Teacher's simple but effective lesson structure

The Lazy structure is based around a basic 'improvement concept' model designed solely to improve learning in the classroom. In its simplest form, the students should experience it as a straightforward process consisting of an on-going (not predetermined) series of 'learning loops' that take on board three simple elements: prepare, do and review.

Prepare, do, review

Beware – this simple principle does not mean it is the three-part lesson in disguise! Rather than having a fixed number of parts to a lesson structure, the learning loops in this model are a series of stages that can be repeated as *many times as necessary* in the lesson. A lesson is never constrained by a preordained number of parts and decided by someone behind a desk building an empire far away from a real classroom.

To add further flexibility, another key principle is that learning is *not a linear activity*. Far from it. Learning in the Lazy Lesson consists of an on-going series of these loops, some planned, some unplanned, and all dictated by what actually happens in the lesson.

What's more, the amount of time spent on each phase is governed by the nature of the learning, not the pages of a national strategy. By repeating the learning loop cycle (prepare, review, do) you are far more inclusive with the class, as learning can be chunked up and reviewed as needed.

The final guiding principle behind the Lazy Lesson structure is to establish independent thinking and learning skills as part of your normal routines. Whilst most schools in the land mention

The Lazy Lesson Structure

Lesson Starter
Energising yet sometimes settling. Use BIG PICTURE and review prior learning.
The Lazy Lesson: students' physical and mental state is prepared for learning.

Lesson End
Re-visit BIG PICTURE.
Preview future learning.
The Lazy Lesson: students are aware of where their learning may go.

Outcome-Focused Delivery
Language used relates to what is expected at the end of the learning.
to be able to describe ... explain ... create ...
The Lazy Lesson: Outcomes are written, explicitly shared with students and revisited throughout the lesson.

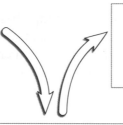

New Learning / Task Introduction
Teacher input to facilitate learning with VAK and Multiple Intelligences.
Establish assessment criteria to enable self, peer and teacher assessment.
The Lazy Lesson: The purpose of a task is linked to outcomes. This is communicated to the students.

Learning Plenary
Discuss, challenge and explore lesson outcomes.
Review outcomes that have been achieved.
The Lazy Lesson: features multi-plenary opportunities engaging the students.

Learning Development
Students work on tasks with strategies in place to avoid dependence on teacher.
The Lazy Lesson: All students are engaged with 'low access – high challenge' tasks.

'independent learning' somewhere on their website, prospectus or school values poster, how many of these schools are actually doing it day in day out in the classroom is quite another matter.

Yet the Lazy Lesson structure lets you develop those thinking and learning skills in *every* lesson. The key: engage your students in a dialogue about learning. At each stage of the learning loop cycle, students review what they are doing and where it is taking them. After just a few weeks you will notice the impact of this on their learning and the growing ability of your students to articulate this clearly. Furthermore, when it comes to occasions such as academic mentoring, subject evenings, parents' evenings or whatever occasion your school uses to discuss learning, you will be able to have a conversation with your students that extends far beyond the traditional remit of how much of the new topic they understand. You might just touch upon the skills needed to be a learner.

Clearly, I am not advocating that the teacher hands out worksheets at the beginning of the lesson that students fill in for the remaining forty minutes whilst you sit there thumbing through the job pages with a cup of coffee. Or worse still, that you plonk your students in front of a PC for the whole lesson to plough their way through some unending multiple choice 'learning software'. This isn't Sweden, after all.

The ideas I put forward in *The Lazy Teacher's Handbook* are all tried and tested practical activities that are enjoyable, engaging, motivating, positive and effective; they are ideas that bring the whole class to life when it comes to learning. And it is the same with this next tranche of ideas in *Whole School Progress the Lazy Way* – great yet simple strategies that hand over much of the process and assessment of learning and progress to the learners, in a professional, effective and unashamedly inspection-friendly way.* What's more, they are ideas that work.

---

* As I am based in England, I have written this book from the perspective of our current inspection process. And the use of the word 'current' indicates (a) I recognise we are in a period of educational change; (b) hope (to allow you to create your own level).

With every new government, change of regime in the inspection process, exam results day or Organisation for Economic Co-operation and Development (OECD) announcement, the topic of 'school improvement' always becomes the focus, with teachers constantly exhorted to be better. For those who don't know because they've never been a teacher (i.e. everyone who is telling teachers how to do their job), the obvious response is that teachers should work harder. But, as teachers, we know that there is only so much carrot and stick we can take, especially if the carrot is being used to beat us as well as the stick. The Lazy Way is our way of saying, stop berating us in this way. We're as professional as hell and we're not going to take it any more. It's about saying, we can't work harder so let's get them, the learners, working harder instead.

And do you know what? When we do things that way everybody benefits. That's the beauty of the Lazy Way.

INTRODUCTION

Introduction

My mother didn't want me to fall off my ladder but, even so, she came pretty close to making it happen. Part way through a flurry of pre-Christmas decorating, and still unable to reconcile the Lazy Way with the 'Y' in DIY (GSETDIFY* not having the same ring to it), I heard the telephone. My wife answered it, eager to have a conversation with a grown-up not whinging about having to paint the hall, and after a few minutes called to me, 'It's your mother. She was wondering if you were making progress with the decorating?'

That was when the wobbles started. She had used the 'P' word. Decorating would never be the same again.

Does she not know, having once been an outstanding teacher ('outstanding' being another word tainted by school inspectors), that such phrases can't be thrown about without inducing an immediate bout of self-reflection, usually followed in my case by self-loathing and a sense of guilt? What if my walls and ceiling were not making as much progress as might be expected? Probably not (there had been some good stuff on the telly). And what happens when you introduce national comparisons? Just how did my walls compare with walls from the top 25% of walls nationally? Not to mention the fact that, at some point, my walls would be sure to figure in some international comparison of wall enhancement practices compiled by the OECD.

Still, at least she didn't say, 'Are you making satisfactory progress, darling?' That would have been time to put down the paintbrushes in total despair and await the arrival of the new uniform and signs rebranding the house 'The B&Q Academy' (where children don't have a tutor room, they have a Homebase. Boom, boom!).

---

*Get Someone Else To Do It For You.

1

Progress is one of the critical words of the modern education era. It's not simply about teaching children, like it used to be. It's not simply about them learning stuff, like it became. It's about how fast they get from A to B and how far that distance is, the further being the better of course. Heaven forfend that a child spends time going nowhere deeply when there's curriculum to cover. Why mine deeply when skimming over the surface gives the impression of going further?

So, the UK's new education framework has progress as a key feature in deciding how good a lesson really is, and I'm not against that. Not entirely. Too many lessons take place where nothing happens. Unless it's a double lesson, in which case – to borrow a phrase from one of the first reviews of Beckett's *Waiting for Godot* – nothing happens twice.

I'm all for pushing children, stretching them, extending them, getting them to do more than they thought they could, more than they thought they even wanted to. And, of course, doing it the Lazy Way – teaching a whole lot less, whilst they sweat the hard stuff. As are thousands of you, judging by the success of *The Lazy Teacher's Handbook*. Despite the hullabaloo over the name and the occasional altercation with traditional teachers who saw it as an affront to their professionalism, many teachers 'got it', built their lessons around the Lazy Way and saw genuine benefits when it came to teaching and learning.

And now that learning alone is not enough, we must turn our lazy attention to progress and ensure that teachers don't fall into the trap of pushing, pulling or otherwise cajoling their learners along the road from A to B but, instead, design lessons that help us maintain our focus on that all-important lazy mantra: you work less so they learn more.

And the same goes for your colleagues whom, along with the students, you may be pushing, pulling and cajoling from A to B (with some keen that you push staff all the way to C for 'competency'). Hence this book also includes some ideas about how to encourage colleagues across the school to make progress. It's what I would call Lazy Leadership of Learning. Although, if we stick to our lazy principle, learning will actually be leading, not you. Simply because if you concentrate on the learning, everything else has a habit of looking after itself.

Making progress is all about making sure the learning – as opposed to the teaching – takes precedence. So it makes sense that the ideas and the philosophy you follow in the classroom are all based on the students progressing more, whilst you do, well, less. In doing so, they become more engaged, happy, proactive and responsible for their learning, and you can turn your considerable experience and skills to doing the tasks in the classroom that only someone with your considerable experience and skills can do. Achieving such a double-whammy outcome does not mean dumbing down, entertaining or avoiding the 'hard yards' of learning. Far from it. Learning can – and should – be challenging. But likewise it doesn't have to be boring, inaccessible and seemingly – or genuinely – pointless. Nor need it be delivered in such a way that ensures the students merely come to school to see the teachers teach. To have students who are engaged, happy, proactive and responsible for their learning and achieve – not to mention regularly exceed – expectations, involves a professionalism on your part way beyond the skill set of someone who confuses teaching with learning.

Such an approach to teaching, with a keen teacherly eye on the tangible progress that every child in your classroom makes each lesson, is what this book is all about. This is what I dedicate my hall ceiling to. Especially the tricky bit going up the stairs.

Chapter 1

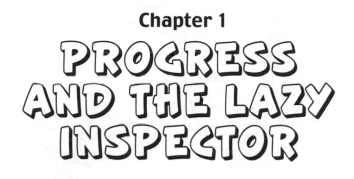

PROGRESS
AND THE LAZY
INSPECTOR

Chapter 1
Progress and the Lazy Inspector

Statisticians would have us believe that it took me thirty minutes to decide what colour to paint the hall. Of course, the decision was obviously my wife's so they got that wrong, but the length of time was about right. Thirty minutes to make a decision you have to live with for quite a while. So, that's about ten minutes more than the Ofsted *Framework for School Inspection from January 2012* says is the minimum amount of time an inspector can sit in your lesson and decide if it's any good or not. If you're any good or not. And by extension your school. Twenty minutes to make an impression. Twenty minutes to sink or swim. Twenty minutes to show learners making progress. And doing it under their own steam.

Of course, you may end up with them in there for a little longer. In many ways it depends which of the two new Ofsted processes you are being put through, either *Ofsted Rapide* (a quick but standard two days) or *Ofsted Lite* (a remote look at your data, a nod, a wink and use of the outstanding logo for another five years).*

Inspectors, used to indulging in the whole – or at least the majority – of a lesson, are now looking for instant evidence with which to make an instant assessment of the learning and progress in your lesson. They consider the progress taking place in the lesson today, as well as indicators as to what has gone on in the past. And it is this instant assessment in your classroom that helps form part of a much longer-lasting judgement about your school.

---

* Please note that Ofsted Lite is only available to outstanding schools which have met all exam performance targets or have AAA credit rating. (OK, the last bit is not true. Yet.)

To do this they will have, although they won't call it this, their own 'evidence of progress wish list' which they will use for judging your lesson within that critical twenty-minute window. The wish list will include:

■ All students demonstrating new learning (preferably independently) and their ability to apply it. This helps Inspector Rapide or Inspector Lite explore the level of challenge for different groups in the class.

■ Conversations between the inspector and the students about their learning and their progress. Simple but deadly questions such as, 'Did you know this before the lesson today?' which of course is laden with inference about pace, challenge and progress.

■ A quick flick through some books to look at levels of work, formative and summative assessment and adherence to school policies, which will help them make a judgement on the leadership of learning as well as progress over time.

■ Evidence not so much of what you *do* but what you *don't* do. After all, it is about the learning not the teaching. This means they play right into the Lazy teacher's hands.

The lesson observation routine will consist of evidence-gathering in these areas, a ticking of the odd box and deciding on a grade, before dashing off to the other side of the school to catch the second half of an Art/Science cross-curricular fusion lesson where rumour has it there is too much emphasis on reflective thinking, student well-being and other such 'tosh'.

And that, in a lazy nutshell, will be it. Possibly years of angst and worry all over in a matter of minutes. Well, twenty minutes in fact. But this book isn't simply designed to make your lessons perfect for when the inspectors arrive (there are other books out there doing that). Like dogs and Christmas or tattoos and stag nights, Lazy Progress isn't just for inspections. It's for every lesson.

A focus on making progress – something that until recently would simply have been referred to as having 'multi-plenaries' – brings with it the all-important principle of checking progress, and this is something that oozes through Lazy Teaching. Being part of the new Ofsted framework just means that you can finally get the credit you deserve. It's not about *you* checking their progress as it was in the old days. It's about *them* checking their progress and, in the process, embedding the learning further still. Which is what it's all for.

And, done the Lazy Way, an inspected lesson is not about you. It's about them.

What does progress look like?

The progress judgement for your lesson covers a number of areas, notably:

- Skills
- Knowledge
- Levels of resilience
- The ability to work independently
- The ability of your learners to articulate their learning

You are judged by the learners' ability to achieve higher levels than their current starting point, something that is assessed both in your lesson and via the data the school holds for a particular key stage. Or, as it was once described to me by someone despairing of my failure to grasp the concept: 'How do I know if it's worth students who want to be better hanging out in your classroom?'

Progress looks and sounds different for each individual you teach. That's why attempting to capture it en masse can at best be clumsy and at worst a disaster – taking over the whole lesson and, ironically, in the process, eliminating the very thing you are trying to measure. Far better to get the students to show progress whilst you demonstrate just how effective being lazy can be. Hence, as with all things done the Lazy Way, your task is to shift the checking of progress from a teacher-led activity to a student-led activity.

It should also be said that routine progress checking is not something that has to be overtly measured and introduced with a musical fanfare heralding a walk-on parade of dancers who didn't quite make the Rio Carnival clutching the golden envelope in which is contained the activity to check progress. Although imagine the approved attendance for SATs or GCSEs if this was adopted for some of the more formal progress checks. It might make choosing an exam board much more entertaining.

It is far better to see progress checking as a process which is blended into the lesson. Indeed, if you were to map assessing progress against the thoughts running through the inspector's head, the current framework and what we know to be effective (i.e. lazy) learning you would have four different categories:

1. Unsatisfactory progress checking – this is characterised by the old three-part lesson whereby the progress check (aka the plenary) came at the end of the lesson and with one minute to go it became apparent to the teacher that nothing had been learnt and they were now yet another lesson nearer to being able to declare the year a write-off. No attempts were made to ascertain what learning had taken place in the lesson and, as a consequence, there was no change of pace or direction as a result of what was (or was not) happening in the lesson.

2. Satisfactory (or possibly worse) progress checking – this is characterised by the teacher stopping the class and any progress (no, the irony will not be lost on the inspector either) to perform a whole-class progress-checking ritual such as 'thumbs up' or a reflective writing activity. This is

promptly followed by more of what was happening just before the class was stopped. Only now they need to be settled again with all the fuss that may involve, so they can get back to making (yes, you have guessed it) some progress. A pointless interjection from which nothing is really gained other than the teacher thinking they have ticked the crucial empty box on the inspector's observation pro forma.

3. Good progress checking – this is characterised by the teacher simply reminding all the students of the progress-checking activity that is built into the lesson as part of the task, before working directly with some students and allowing others to get on with it themselves. Students could be:

    ■ Asking questions of each other.

    ■ Recalibrating the level of difficulty of the task by choosing a challenge with increased difficulty for the next part of the lesson.

    ■ Reviewing the marking feedback from their peers or the teacher to make sure they are acting on the comments.

    ■ Self-assessing their progress with each of the different success criteria.

    ■ Reflecting what their own 'must–should–could', is in order to make an action plan for the remainder of the lesson.

    As a result of the progress check, the behaviours for learning look and sound different. Learning is likely to have increased not only during the progress check but also afterwards as well. After all, making progress is about learning, not jumping through Ofsted hoops.

4. Outstanding progress checking – this is characterised by a *willingness of the students themselves* to take responsibility for their progress checking as they understand and can articulate why being reflective links in with being an effective learner.

Tasks are blended into the students' learning as opposed to the teacher's teaching. The task becomes invisible and develops into more of a learning–coaching conversation between learners or an internal dialogue within each individual learner. Clearly students who need support in this are assisted either by their peers or an adult in the room. Unintended learning is also captured that may or may not relate to the lesson outcomes but this is still used by the teacher to further the progress of the students. This is the mother lode!

It should be noted that such a rich vein of golden learning takes time, commitment and confidence from you to make it happen. It is a journey (that becomes increasingly lazy for you) during which the students develop and acquire the necessary skills; although, paradoxically, the starting point and the end point are much the same: students who stare at you with disbelief and wear a blank look if you ask them about the importance of reviewing learning. The subtle difference is that by the end of the journey, the bemusement will simply be your students wondering why you even bothered asking such an obvious question.

Over a number of lessons, the students will become increasingly happy performing their new role of checking progress, especially when they see the benefits for their learning. And the more colleagues who join you, the better and more efficient they will become. Furthermore, what is important is that for the 0.1% of times your lessons are observed, you will now be presenting some neatly packaged evidence for the observer. Oh yes, and for the remaining 99.9% of lessons you will be thinking, 'I wish someone was here to see the progress my students are making.'

It's amazing what a lazy twist can do to your thinking!

Characteristics that enable progress to flourish

Our own classroom experience tells us that there are some common characteristics and behaviours that make all the difference when it comes to embedding learning and showcasing progress. Although we all have our favourites, here is my list with, as you would expect, a lazy theme running through it.

Six characteristics of learning in which outstanding progress thrives (and that you would especially want to show off to an inspector)

1. Teachers allow time for students to think and create learning over and above that linked to the lesson outcome, often responding to unintended but valuable learning opportunities.

2. Teachers reduce their role to a minimum so as not to dominate the learning and thereby allow learners maximum ownership of their learning and free time for independent study.

3. Learners show high levels of engagement, respect, collaboration and cooperation to and with everyone and everything in the room, recognising that it is not just the teacher who can facilitate learning.

4. Learners design and create their own learning experience simply by being given choice in any task by the teacher. This results in greater ownership, and subsequently greater progress, without any additional input from the teacher.

5. Learning is realigned as a result of self, peer-to-peer or teacher-led progress checks to maximise the effectiveness of the students.

6. The learners and the teacher look happy, share a laugh and enjoy the lesson, having a mutual respect for each other's work.

Warning! Checklists for teaching are fraught with inaccuracies and have a nasty tendency to leave you feeling overwhelmed and under-skilled as you chase a tick in every box. Hence this checklist, like all others, should be:

1. Treated with caution.

2. Never be seen as a 'Thou shalt complete all of these'. It is a list of language and phrases aimed at trying to describe the atmosphere in the room when we know all is shipshape and Bristol fashion when it comes to learning.

3. Amended to reflect what 'outstanding' looks like with each of the different groups, classes and individuals you teach.

4. Regarded not as a recipe but as 'serving suggestion'. You can have all the cookbooks in the world but unless you are tasting, smelling and experimenting as you go along, you will never produce what the photo of the meal suggests you should.

Warnings aside, simply bear in mind that there is one crucial principle that is common both to being outstanding in an Ofsted way and effective in a Lazy Way: the responsibility for the checking of progress lies with the students themselves.

Moving towards progress checking in a Lazy Way

At the heart of the Lazy Way is the idea of learners leading their own learning. And checking for progress is no different. If you have already made headway with Lazy Teaching you will know how important it is to explain your pedagogy to the students. It is a lot easier to engage with something if you know the rationale behind it. Checking for progress is no different. The way I do it in my lessons is to describe them merely as games (which, on occasion, are single player) that:

■ Are designed to operate in parallel with the main learning activity. A side dish to the main course, the sag aloo to the chicken tikka masala, to continue the culinary theme (I must remember to eat before I start writing), into which you dip every now and then and which will be completed by the end of the lesson, but is never something you stop the whole meal for to lick the dish clean.

■ Add additional challenge to stretch your learners and prove what they can achieve.

■ Act as an opportunity for you to realign their learning to the main task to make sure they remain on track for the targets they have set.

The logic in presenting progress checkers as games is not so much that I believe in 'edutainment' but more the principle that once a game is learnt we set ourselves up for life. In the same way that if you were to give a group of people a box of Monopoly or Connect Four they would be able to get on and play the game, learning can be like that as well. But only if we use the same approaches that students have already learnt rather than being up all night thinking, 'How can I teach that?'

Embed the ideas into your Lazy Lesson structure so the students and you can both see progress in all its forms oozing out all over the learning environment. And when that's happening, the inspector can become lazy and will not even need to stay beyond that twenty-minute window and will not bother you again. And that really would be outstanding progress.

Chapter 2

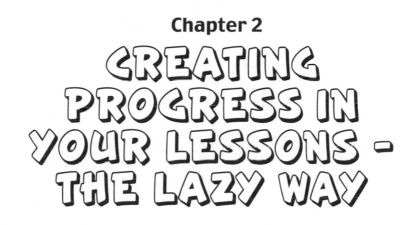

Chapter 2

Creating Progress In Your Lessons – The Lazy Way

There comes a time in every teacher's life when circumstances mean that your existence might just include something else in it during the evening other than marking and lesson planning. It might be children, training with the hockey team or a disillusioned partner who you spot typing up an advert seeking 'term-time companionship' – offers from non-teachers only, please.

I know over the years I could claim two of three, and I don't play hockey. So with my work–life balance tweaked and as a proud advocate of the Lazy Way, I can always be persuaded to mount a defence for the statement:

You can plan an amazing lesson with loads of progress in less than three minutes and still be considered as a professional.

Now, before such an admission leads to another letter from the irate woman who wrote to me upon seeing *The Lazy Teacher's Handbook* in her staff library saying I had let the profession down and was unprofessional for advocating being lazy (quite clearly she had neither read the book nor knew anything of me as a professional), let me explain the caveats I make prior to commencing the defence:

1. We know our subject content. This may be an assumption that is ill founded but either you do have a First Class honours degree from a Russell Group university or, in the current climate, would be wise to pretend to have. In other words, subject content is not an issue (other than sometimes knowing too much).

2. We know our classes. As part of your role as a teacher you spend time observing the learning behaviours of your students to try and understand how they like to learn and when they progress the most.

3. Err ... that's it.

Just two caveats which, if in place, mean I would surely win any debate about lesson planning. And remember, that means lessons that include loads of progress. My confidence in the debate stems from working out that there are three key questions that underpin the Lazy Lesson planning for progress:

1. **What do the students need to do?**

   No point planning for something that is not needed – you can rely on the class to come up with lots of wonderful learning distractions, you don't need to plan them.

2. **Based on what I have seen and heard, what choice of activities will enable the students to best make progress in 75% of the lesson time?**

   Too often planning starts with us thinking, 'Right, what do we need to cover?', which as a phrase is not exactly awe inspiring, especially if replicated in the classroom. With that mindset we often indulge far too much of the lesson in teacher time, leaving little opportunity for progress because the whole lesson has been about us, not them. What if you changed that around and started with them – you might just be surprised.

3. **What do I need to do in the remaining 25% of lesson time to make this happen?**

   The skill of the Lazy teacher is to work out how that is going to happen. Besides, having more time is simply not an option. And as you contemplate the non-negotiable nature of that last sentence, it would be completely natural for you to recall all the strategies that reduce unnecessary teacher talk in the lesson, such as students knowing the processes underlying pedagogical activities, effective use of ICT to recap instructions and use of prior knowledge. We don't need loads of teacher time in every lesson. The better we are, the less time we need.

And this is where both this book and its slightly older brother come into play as they provide you with the data bank of pedagogical activities that demonstrate progress. All you have to do is choose one for each stage of the Lazy Lesson structure (see page xii).

You will soon develop a number of templates that work. All that changes is the content you and the students wrap around your pedagogical framework. And if you want to take a lead on developing the Lazy planning ethos across your school, why not share lesson plans with colleagues? It might just be that your group work lesson, topic launch lesson, coursework lesson or assessment lesson is structured in a similar way. All you need to do is observe your groups and make sure you personalise lesson plans to your own situation. After all, as it is with rivers, you never step in the same class twice.

Planning lessons during which all students move forwards really does not require lots of time. Honestly. OK, admittedly, it is one of those things that the better you are at it, the quicker you are at it, but that will happen in a matter of weeks. And, after a term, you'll be training others and have a queue of people wanting to know the secret.

So, there really is no need to sit there, despairing of your career choice, worrying about planning and progress into the early hours. Or until the doorbell rings, proving that your partner's advert did work ...

Twelve ideas that mean students make progress with their learning

1. Top tenuous*

Thanks to Radio 2 DJ Chris Evans for inspiring this one. How can the learners link themselves to the topic they are studying – however tenuous it may be? By making a link between themselves and the learning it might just become that little bit more relevant. So, be it the Romans, photosynthesis, van Gogh or making a moisture detector, what's their tenuous link? The students might just be more involved than they think.

Some of the less tenuous and direct links resulted in me being amazed to discover that the father of one of my students was a friend of Thomas Friedman, author of the international best-seller *The World is Flat*. Such a connection triggered a renaissance in the student's love of geography and became a basis to speak to the father, resulting in him becoming a governor. Other colleagues will cite endless occasions where we have made contact with guest speakers or had artefacts loaned to us just by asking the students how they are connected to the learning.

And whilst the headlines are always exciting, everyone can make a link in a few steps, which in itself provides great lateral thinking skills as well as reminding them that the learning always involves them. After all, we are all linked by six degrees of separation. Apart from The Three Degrees. Who ironically are linked in one.

2. Progress snakes that bite!

Ask students to choose a word that best describes what has been new to them today (in other words, how have they pro-

---

*This idea comes from Andy Lean at the Marlowe Academy, Ramsgate.

gressed!). It may be a skill, knowledge or even an emotion. Offer a free choice of words or, to add more challenge (but be careful not to impede their ability to articulate progress), restrict the language they can use by randomly selecting a letter and asking students to come up with a word beginning with just that letter. After some thinking time, invite every student to say their word in a non-stop, continuous sweep around the room. In this way you get a range of words, with some repeated as the students summarise their learning. This gives you the 'snake' part of the game. From that you could record frequently occurring words, then go back and ask the students to explore, by means of some structured talk, what the people around them have said.

You could also play the 'bite' part of the game, which is merely a reference to any additional challenges that can be bolted on. Examples could be:

- The last person repeats the most frequently occurring word (most effective when used with single letter responses).

- The last person has to select a different word to all those previously said.

- You ask if anyone can recall the words of five other people.

- Choose any five words from the group and ask students to link them back to the topic you are studying.

- 5-3-1 bite! This involves students choosing *five* words they have heard and describing them. They then explain what any *three* of the five mean. Finally they write a question to which the answer will be *one* of the words from the three they have explained.

If you are running out of 'bite' options, just ask the students to develop some for you. All of the activities are about reviewing and making permanent the progress in the lesson.

Furthermore, an expectation that progress is going to take place creates a heightened sense of learning as well as enjoyment in the class.

3. If today was a ...

... flower, what would it be? If today was a colour, what would it be? If this book was a vegetable, what would it be? (Hopefully not rotten!)

This one is a classic reminder that we need to present learning as low access and high challenge, without the fear of the right–wrong trapdoor. Let go of the need for all of the answers to be the 'right ones'. Just see what happens if, just for a minute, you stop teaching the syllabus. Progress comes in all shapes and sizes and it is sometimes these sorts of questions that unlock progress for the very first time and let you see that it takes different questions to unlock different people.

4. What has this lesson got in common with the lesson before?

When you chat to students, especially older ones, it is interesting how they compartmentalise their learning into subjects and make very few connections across the curriculum. This idea helps them bridge the gap and in a way become lazy learners by seeing what skills and knowledge can be reused.

For this task they simply make a connection between the previous lesson and what they are going to be doing in the current lesson. Answers need not be restricted to knowledge. This is a good technique for exploring transferable learning skills. You might even want to enhance the process by asking a colleague to pre-expose them in their lesson to key ideas from your lesson. This subliminal reinforcement is a great way to give a clear message to students that the staff are all working together. After all, isn't the students' progress in any one subject the responsibility of everyone at the school? Who knows who unlocked the thinking that triggered the progress?

5. **What has the lesson got in common with the job I want?**

As above, but with a careers twist, making the link between your lesson and how it can help them to fulfil future ambitions (which improves motivation).

6. **MANAP (Make A New Acronym Please)**

In the current day and age, students with the ability to make up and decipher acronyms will go far, and for those who are considering a career in education, this task counts as work experience. Quite simply, ask them to develop acronyms to help them remember key bits of learning and lock in the progress made.

Not only do they need to synthesise the key points of your lesson with accuracy and brevity, they are also looking to choose words to make a meaningful acronym, so it counts as literacy too. Back of the net! Oh yes, and they have just started to tap into the world of lazy revision by making resources as they go along – it takes a whole lot less effort to remember an acronym than a great body of text.

For example, in maths it is common to use BIDMAS (**B**rackets, **I**ndices (**p**owers and **r**oots), **D**ivision, **M**ultiplication, **A**ddition, **S**ubtraction). Or in PE you could use FITT (**F**requency, **I**ntensity, **T**ime, **T**ype) to help remember the characteristics of individual training programmes.

We can use acronyms to help show progress with more than just learning: they are also useful to help devise a kit list for the more forgetful in your class who should always BAPPEL before school: (**B**ook bag, **A**pple (or snack), **P**encil case, **PE** kit, **L**unchbox).

7. Would I lie to you?

'Maybe yes, maybe no' was my honest answer following a great discussion with one of my classes on the topic of whether it is ever acceptable to lie. However, for this exercise, assume that lying through your teeth is acceptable behaviour, especially as it proves to the students the progress they have made with learning.

Ask your students to read through an extended piece of text and memorise two true statements and one false one. They then work the room, sharing their truths and untruths with each other and trying to catch one another out. Feel free to join in as well – you should always trust a teacher, shouldn't you?

'Would I lie to you?' is a really effective way to engage students and can be applied to any task where you want information absorbed and you need a purpose at the end of it; not just simply, 'You need to know this, read it and make notes'. It means that students are more focused and, as such, when you give them less time to make their notes, they can do this quicker and more effectively having played with the information rather than drifting into copying passages from the book.

8. Progress Paparazzi

It is inevitable that you won't see everything that happens in your lesson, which is one of the reasons why the feedback from lesson observations can come as such an eye opener. The reality is that there is too much going on, be it progress or otherwise. So it makes perfect sense to engage others in helping to collect evidence of all those effective learning behaviours you would otherwise have missed.

Nominate Progress Paparazzi to be on the lookout for students making great progress, contributing to learning or thinking creatively. To give the paparazzi credibility, grant them the right to recommend their peers for merits, house points, sweets, chart stickers or whatever the rewards may be. You might even have 'The Learner's Learner Award' or 'Most Valuable Learner'. Or imagine if each adult who entered the room was made to hand out one discretionary 'Visitor's Badge of Honour' each time they came into your classroom, to reward something that took their (guided) fancy in the room.

With students allowed to praise and reward each other, this is a great activity for building collaborative trust and enhanced ownership of learning, which is crucial if progress is to flourish. What's more, the more eyes that are looking for good work, the more that work will be spotted and rewarded, thereby addressing the perennially demotivating problem of children whose day-in, day-out learning is so rarely recognised.

Oh yes, and you can equip your paparazzi with as much ICT as you wish, supplementing their own all-seeing eyes with video cameras and MP3 recorders. After all, the camera and the paparazzi never lie!

9. **If the following were having breakfast what might they be talking about?**

Sometimes progress flows when we reframe the learning and take it right out of context. Removing what students expect us to say and do often gives unexpectedly brilliant answers back. A great idea that moves us in that direction is the Breakfast Club, something that has many different ways of being delivered, from a live drama production through to cartoon strips or a simple class discussion.

To start with, choose some characters, or indeed items, relevant to the topic you are studying and simply imagine they were having a conversation over breakfast (a culinary concept which may need explaining to some of your students for whom breakfast is a Red Bull and a packet of Quavers on the way to school).

The characters might be discussing plots, their thoughts on other people or how they think the story of their life might unfold. Once your students get the hang of this one you can push them further – those at the breakfast table do not necessarily have to be from the same period of time, topic or life form. The more eclectic the mix of ingredients, the better – like muesli.

10. Your portfolio of learning investments

Please note, the value of learning can go up and down and past performance is not necessarily an indicator of future performance. Your interest rate can vary over time and you should be aware that your interest rates will determine the future pay-out. Terms and conditions apply. Full details can be seen on school reports ...

Or so an advert might read if the advertising standards people got hold of some marketing material encouraging students to invest in learning. That said, asking students to record what they are investing in their learning, and similarly how much they are getting back, is a great exercise to help focus their minds on progress and motivation.

By asking them at intervals over the term to plot their input (what they are going to contribute to the lesson, to their learning, to school life, etc.) and plot their return (how they feel, the progress they are making, the grades they are getting, etc.) you are helping them better understand the simple correlation between inputs and outputs when it comes to progress. *They* need to play a part, not just you, especially if you are sticking to your Lazy teaching principles.

11. Prove it!

A great way to start thinking, and a subsequent debate, in your classroom is by offering statements that the whole class has to prove. For example, you could get everyone to prove that light bulbs suck in dark as opposed to giving off light.*

Another variation is to organise groups against each other by setting them slightly different challenges or having them take opposing views. Examples might include:

■ Prove that your Achilles tendon is more important than your hamstring.

■ Prove that the Romans were nastier than the Vikings.

■ Prove that vinegar is more useful than lemon juice.

■ Prove that Enid Blyton is a better writer than William Shakespeare.

12. Lazy surfing

Technology continues to be the Lazy teacher's friend as it offers instant, reusable and often free ideas to make learning more accessible. And, in my experience, as soon as learning becomes accessible, the students develop the appetite for it to become more challenging – which is when the progress really kicks in!

The sites that follow are just a selection of ones that I regularly source from my colleague Mark Anderson, who is the pedagogy behind a very useful blog (www.ictevangelist.com). This site is an up-to-date teacher reference guide of simple-to-use websites and apps that have a proven and immediate impact in the classroom. Many of the students will already be familiar with them. And if they aren't, simply give them a little steer to the website and they will do the rest. (The Lazy teacher knows full well that, when it comes to ICT, everything

---

*Although you might need a better example as we know this to be true. If you watch a game of sport at night, the floodlights suck all the darkness out of the stadium so you can see what is going on. Turn the floodlights off, the stadium fills with darkness again. Clearly true. Now, yer sun, that's obviously the biggest dark catcher in the universe. It can even work through clouds, but interestingly not through the earth itself. This is why it falls dark when we rotate.

is better when we let the students get on with the learning, not us.)

Five websites that promote progress via ICT

1. **Present your case with Museum Box – http://museumbox. e2bn.org/index.php**

    The anti-slavery campaigner, Thomas Clarkson, was the inspiration for this website. In the late eighteenth century he collected evidence in a chest to support the case he was making to end slavery. This site replicates Clarkson's approach with very simple tools so students can build up an argument or description of an event, person or historical period by placing e-evidence into a virtual box. This box then becomes the students' evidence treasure trove and basis of their project or presentation to share with the class in a version of 'show and tell'.

    The approach encourages greater progress from students as they are more inclined to discuss items, pose questions and say how they feel, as opposed to rattling off some bullet points researched from Wikipedia and pasted into another 'PowerPointless' presentation.

    It has been used in several contexts with ideas such as:

    - What items would you put in a box to describe your life?

    - What items would you put in a box to indicate that it belonged to a centurion?

    - What evidence would you store in a box to show that chopping down the rainforests was harmful/not harmful?

    Students can collect e-newspaper articles, pictures, videos of them performing a play or whatever it is they think helps to build their argument. It is all collected in one easy-to-use website that is password protected. This is a great concept that weaves together awe and wonder, independent research, discussion and debating skills, as well as tapping into the desire to collect stuff. A far cry from simply printing off the first thing that appears at the top of a web search.

2. Grab a free autocue – www.cueprompter.com

If you are staging an assembly, practising public speaking or acting out your learning via a chat show, for example, then this little gadget adds an extra real-life dimension to what is happening.

A twist for the Lazy but evil teacher is to set up your group to perform a chat show and then replicate the infamous scenario that saw a taxi driver arrive at the BBC in London but, inexplicably, ends up speaking live on the news about consumers and technology. Brilliant! Simply let the autocue deliver the news that all the roles and characters have changed, but they still have to carry on as it is, after all, 'live' TV (maniacal laugh) …

3. It's how big? – www.howbigreally.com

A great site for generating 'Oooh! Whodathought!' awe and wonder, as well as linking subjects together for some cross-curricular work. It simply personalises the mapping of various historical, environmental and current events to a location of your choice, using a postcode. So if you want to see how long a Spitfire runway was in comparison to your school grounds or how big the moon is compared to where you live, this is the site for you. (And it makes a change from using Wales as the universal standard of comparison as the media always seem to do.)

One of the many projects that has come out of the site includes estimating the size of the Gulf of Mexico oil spill in 2010 and putting in bids for how much it would cost to clean it up at £100 per square kilometre. Maths meets geography: progress on the cross-curricular numeracy front!

4. **Are you talking to me? – www.reallusion.com/crazytalk, www.voki.com, Puppet Pals app and X Factor Announcer app**

Still a real favourite with the students and an opportunity for you to not even have to talk, as you can get someone else to do it for you! The common aspect of all these pieces of software (that range from free to £40) is the ability to get someone else delivering the lesson by means of a talking avatar or animation. It frees you up to observe learning and frees up the students from unnecessarily having to listen to you repeating instructions to the whole class when just a few want clarification.

So, if you want a frog talking about his journey from being a tadpole, Winston Churchill talking about the Second World War or Mona Lisa taking an art lesson, these are the software packages for you. Likewise, if you want the booming, distinctive tones of Peter Dickson, the X Factor announcer, welcoming your class or telling them 'It is, time, to PACK AWAYYYY' then the X Factor Announcer app is just what you need.

A word of warning: don't become too despondent when they pay more attention to a frog than they do to you. Instead, feel smug at how lazy you are being, whilst giving the students minimum time listening to you and maximum time to make progress.

5. **Create ICT 'How to …' movies with Jing – www.techsmith.com/Jing**

It may well be the case that your contribution to the development of ICT in your students is that one-off lesson which involves you reserving the computer room months in advance so as to get one over on the hotshot teacher down the corridor who normally books up every available free lesson. Or maybe you're grappling with a newfangled bit of kit that has suddenly appeared in your classroom, such as a tablet PC or even an iPad, which you are supposed to know how to use instantly, even though the only way you can get the time display on your microwave at home to stop flashing is to unplug it.

Either way, what we need to resist with ICT is the urge to waste time explaining something that we know little about to a group of people who clearly know far more than we do, and whose younger siblings could set the microwave timer with their eyes closed.

Instead, put your lazy hat on and get the students to create a pre-recorded 'how to ...' video using Jing, complete with screen shots and movies. Students can play them back over and over again to ensure they 'get it', and once they're made you can use them with other classes in truly lazy style.

This is just a flavour of what is currently being used in classrooms and many of you reading this will have your own favourite websites list. What unites them all (or at least should unite them) is that they all serve to help us make the lazy shift from teaching to learning. And, in doing so, cut down our explanation time in the classroom to a minimum, which frees up those who, are able to learn and means we can target those who, momentarily, may need some extra teaching. Of the lazy variety, of course.

Indeed, Lazy Teaching may just be the tip of the iceberg when it comes to learning and technology. There may be more truth than we care to acknowledge in the title of Ian Gilbert's book, *Why Do I Need A Teacher When I've Got Google?*

Lazy language that maximises progress

It seems obvious, but what we say in the classroom has a massive impact on learning. And then there is the question of quality, not to mention the issue so many teachers have over quantity. If we want to maximise progress the Lazy Way we need to work on improving the former and reducing the latter. In other words, we need to develop our Lazy teacher script. So, in a learning style of your choice, go away and learn your new lines, as would any great actor. This way you can continue your antithetical role as the principal lead who only ever performs from the wings.

The Lazy teacher's script redux

1. **Update your terminology**

   Like most long running shows, you need to remain a little bit topical to keep the audience interested. So when you say words like 'PowerPoint', do you actually mean PowerPoint? Whilst it might be the only software you know, the students may be able to produce something bigger and better using something else. Be careful, therefore, not to speak in a way that keeps it simple for you, but too simple for them. Try saying 'multimedia presentation' and see what comes back instead. You might find that a few different words will unlock a whole load of talent.

2. **Importance of pre-exposure – the EWAP classroom**

   Being aware of how the work they we are doing this lesson links to the learning that follows is crucial to maximising students' progression. It means that they are undertaking their work with a purpose. When this happens, and students are industriously setting about their work knowing where it is leading, you have created your EWAP learning time. And

EWAP simply stands for – Everything With A Purpose. EWAP has a considerable bearing on the amount of progress achieved in a lesson, as the students are clear that the task they are working on now is clearly linked to the success they will have with the next or future tasks (and even, dare I say it, exams). With the purpose clear, reluctantly or otherwise, the students know they have to crack on – and crack on they do.

For example, rather than having students sit through a DVD and then answer a series of questions, let them have the questions up front. Better still, let them have a go at answering them up front, combining pre-exposure with predicting skills. Better still – and even lazier – get them to come up with questions both before and after watching the DVD that they can pose to other people, and you can nab for future use. Such activities also help avoid the embarrassing silence when students are asked that line beloved of Ofsted inspectors, 'Do you know why you are doing this?'

3. Great expectations

Whilst each lesson will naturally have its own feel and energy, there is something to be said for setting the scene about expectations for the lesson. Set high expectations for everyone from the off by talking about challenge, progression and what will be achieved, using their past performance as the (positive) starting point:

- ■ 'Based on how well you performed last lesson, I am looking for the same again plus 10%, as that will mean we are … (insert suitable phrase, e.g. cooking on gas!).'

- ■ 'This work is normally not covered until next year but, seeing as you are making such good progress, I think you are ready for it now. But I will need you to focus.'

- ■ 'I need you to work beyond what you think you are capable of. I have faith you can do it.'

And when you need to correct someone's approach, you simply remind them of what was expected at the start of the lesson and, more often than not, they will self-coach and correct their behaviour.

4. Tapas learning

Not for you, but for the student. The notion of having a choice instantly encourages students to think about the work – even if it is about how little they can get away with (lazy teachers is one thing; lazy students is a different thing altogether). So present your work with options, perhaps mirroring what might happen in an assessment or exam (e.g. Choose one question from section A, two from section B and one from section C). Your skill, as a teacher, is to design questions in such a way that it does not matter which ones they answer.

Likewise, offer choice in the order in which they can answer the questions or complete the tasks. They know they have to get it all done; how that happens is up to them. By presenting the tasks 'tapas' style, you offer some variety to the normal 'set menu' approach students usually receive. And who knows, they might come up with a new combination that suits them much better than anything you can cook up. After all, people plot all sorts of routes from A to B, believing they have the path that they can progress along the quickest. Your students will be no different.

5. The silent movie

If it's good enough for the Oscars, then it's good enough for your classroom. There are plenty of ways to encourage great progress that don't involve the Lazy teacher opening his or her mouth at all. Thinking templates, effective learning behaviours, posters or pictograms of our favourite learning tools on display all do the job very well in my experience. Instead of having to remember your lines, simply point the students to the display. You talk less and they begin to learn the script for themselves.

So, with that brief smorgasbord of lazy techniques complete (I really must get something to eat) make sure you waste no time in putting them to use in improving learning. Any delay may see you exposed to the perils of teaching more, yet achieving less. And if it is progress you are after, this is a trap to avoid at all costs.

Sustaining Lazy Progress in the lesson

It was a simple request: please would I pop out and buy some tomatoes. And don't forget the Bag for Life. Or at least, it seemed a simple request. But life, like learning and the Rotastak Spaghetti Junction Hamster Cage, is full of unexpected twists and turns. Not to mention hurdles, obstacles and those special sorts of challenges that come from one minute feeling smug because you've got a decent parking space on a busy shopping day, and the next minute you're standing in the fruit and veg aisle of Tesco mouthing silently the perennial Spike Milligan question, 'What are we going to do now?'

You see, I wasn't sent off looking for any old tomatoes. That would have been far too simple. Instead, I had been sent in search of the elusive Pomodoro di Pachino, a key ingredient for a meal my wife was preparing for our special dinner guests. And I had been entrusted with one task – that of hunting and gathering this delicacy. What could possibly go wrong?

Whether it was some old family rivalry deep in the Sicilian countryside that had affected supply, or inefficiency by some disaffected teenager being asked to work for nothing to gain valuable work skills and 'show willing', I will never know. All I did know was that there was a Pomodoro di Pachino-shaped hole looking at me from the shelf. Like a soup kitchen in a cold snap, the Pomodoro di Pachino was out stock. What are we going to do now?

If I were to follow the lead of my students when faced with such a moment, then I would have simply implemented the recurrent 'stuck strategy' beloved of all young learners:

1. Freeze.

2. Put your hand up.

3. Enthusiastically shout, 'I'm stuck!'

4. Await assistance.

5. Engage those around you in conversation about something unrelated to the work.

6. Repeat as needed to fill up a whole lesson.

Remember to alternate which hand is raised so as not to lose all the blood from one arm, as this results in you making various noises intimating you are seconds from death and drawing the teacher over to you, which is obviously not the aim of the strategy. When the teacher finally arrives, the learner may even receive an apology for the delay in getting to them, which ensures the student is in the driving seat from the off. If the teacher ever has the temerity to ask them what they have been doing all this time, the reply 'Waiting for you, Sir' is a hard one to fight, especially as the guilt starts to rear its head, often leading to another mumbled apology from the teacher.

Whilst such tactics work in the classroom (and even raise their heads on INSET days I've noticed) they are pretty futile in a supermarket. The 'get someone else to sort your problem out for you' tactic lasted as long as it took the 'Team Leader – Fruit and Veg' to offer a cursory 'Sorry mate, out of stock' before he walked off, leaving me to contemplate the fast-developing Pomodoro di Pachino-gate incident a little more.

On the point of tearing up my Clubcard in frustration, it suddenly dawned on me that 'Team Leader – Fruit and Veg' had done me a massive favour (and should by now be hard at work on the *Lazy*

Team Leader – Fruit and Veg Handbook). Unable to solve my dilemma, even if he had wanted to, he was simply affording me the opportunity to think for myself and thus avoid the trap that so many young people fall into, that of learnt helplessness.

In our classrooms we need to learn from 'Team Leader – Fruit and Veg' and adopt a similar approach with our students. This is Lazy Teaching at its best and will guarantee that young people make progress, almost despite themselves. When 'I'm stuck, Sir' is met, in the right way and with the right intent, with 'Is that right? Well, what are *you* going to do about it?' then we are really doing our learners a favour and setting them up for a lifetime of being able to deal with problems, crises and everything else life will, sooner or later, throw at them. And, maybe, when they're faced with a serious tomato incident they will thank you for it.

Below are some great lazy strategies aimed at prolonging the time that students can work independently, without that 'I'm stuck' hand going up.

'Help, I'm stuck' – lazy ideas that extend independent learning

As I mentioned earlier, language is really important in our classroom, but due to the intensity of delivering a learning experience we quite often do not hear some of the phrases that we use. It is really worth recording one of your lessons to pick up on the phrases and verbal mannerisms, tics even, you may have developed. Some of them may not only be clichéd but also indirectly guide the students to become dependent on you, as opposed to relying on their own initiative a great deal more. How many times have you found yourself saying something along the lines of: 'OK, you all know what to do, so make a start now. Have a go at the questions and, if you get stuck, just put your hand up and I'll come and help'?

No! We have just legitimised the very thing that they might want to do. Namely, nothing. So, here is a selection of other phrases and actions to use when greeted with the phrase 'Help, I'm stuck' which mean that you can combine Lazy Teaching with outstanding learning.

Lazy (but effective) things to say in response to 'Help, I'm stuck' so progress does not come to a shuddering halt

1. **'OK, so do something different.'**

   Students need to build up resilience and lose the culture of, 'If at first you don't succeed, put your hand up and wait'. It never ceases to amaze me how much young people persevere, trying different things over and over again, when they are stuck attempting a new skateboard move or reaching the next level on a computer game. They just don't seem to bring that perserverance into the classroom.

   In emphasising the 'different', it is good to role model that learning does not have to be linear. Different minds will plot many a different route through the problem. Hence this phrase acts as both guidance and encouragement, reassuring them that it is OK to be tackling the work in a different way to the person they are sitting next to.

2. **'Well, imagine you were someone who was not stuck – what would they do?'**

   This needs to be delivered with a smile and, although you have asked a question, you may choose not to hang around for the answer as it may drag you into a conversation which is merely an anti-progress strategy. The other reason to walk away is that the student may well finish your one-liner (a sure sign that strategies are embedded) with something equally as sarcastic, which it might be best not to hear. After all, you did start it!

3. **'If you could go home when you have finished that bit of work what would you do?'**

Students sometimes say they are stuck because the end goal is seemingly too far away or is not that desirable, such as finishing a worksheet about something they have no interest in. Reframing the end goal with something they find appealing, for example going home, can spark them into life and break the cycle of 'I'm stuck, I'm bored, I'm bored because I'm stuck ...'

N.B. This is intended to be a humorous question, so works best with ridiculous non-deliverable rewards, such as going home early, £1 million, a Ferrari and so on. It is not about offering a lollipop for every piece of work.

4. **'What have you forgotten to do?'**

This one is more often than not followed by the student saying, 'Oh yes, I forgot to ...' as they are prompted to recall your instructions, look at someone else's work or look at the wall display for guidance. It is simply another way of refocusing them and letting the progress continue. This works really well if you want students to follow or discover a sequential step of instructions in a formula, a recipe or design work.

5. **'Think what the answer is then work backwards to where you are now.'**

It seems totally illogical to make someone skip to the answer, especially if they are stuck, but I have found this one works really well with discursive or opinion-based writing. Often students get caught up in the arguments and lose sight of the end goal, which means progress comes to a halt. Giving them a rocket boost to the end offers a sense of satisfaction and slight relief that the task is 'completed', making the back-filling all that little bit easier.

6. **'Imagine you were to give it a go as somebody else – what could you do?'**

    Sometimes students mask their insecurities and embarrassment about having a go and getting something wrong with the claim that they are stuck, when really they are not. This question works to overcome that awkwardness by detaching the suggestions that are made from the pupil and instead giving their ownership to an imaginary person. It is surprisingly effective in getting students to have a go. You can encourage more than one idea by saying, 'And what else might they do?'

7. **'OK, do it wrong so we have something to work with.'**

    The principle behind this is that you need to get under the skin of their thinking before you can offer help. What's more, because students are not used to deliberately getting something wrong, they reapply themselves to the task of trying to get it right. It shouldn't work. But it does. Especially when there is a culture in the room that everyone will achieve and, in the end, they will all discover how to get it right.

8. **'OK, find someone who can explain it better than me as I've had a go and clearly failed.'**

    If your self-esteem has taken a bit of a battering, there is nothing like a needy group of students to make you feel wanted. Well, for a few minutes anyway. Yet by downplaying the role you play and the skills you have, you can instantly promote other people and resources in the room that can help.

    N.B. If they ask you to have another go, remind them that doing the same thing and expecting a different result is neither a good teaching nor a good learning strategy. It is, however, a sign of madness.

9. **'OK, what did you do successfully last time you were stuck on a problem like this?'**

    This is just a simple memory jogger to tap into previous successful strategies for sustaining progress. And with a bit of thinking time, it may be that the students can recall strategies from across all their lessons, not just yours. And, of course, the comment can be flipped to begin a process of elimination: 'OK, what didn't work last time you were stuck on a problem like this?'

10. 'Well done, now the real learning begins. I look forward to what you are going to choose to do!'

'I'm stuck' is sometimes said with a hint of resignation or embarrassment in the student's voice. Turn this into something to celebrate and you are reframing the situation from one of despair to one of excitement and anticipation. Far from thinking less of them, you are actually praising them in anticipation of what they are going to do. And, as with all these phrases, eliminate the possibility of them asking you for help by finishing your sentence whilst walking away, looking back and offering a smile. It might seem harsh, but progress sometimes involves tough love; just make sure you smile. Being stuck and learning is, after all, meant to be a happy experience.

11. 'OK, record why you are stuck and what you have tried in your diary and move on.'

It transpires, from the groups I have tried this with, that building up a 'diary of being stuck' is less enjoyable than persevering with the piece of work you are stuck on. So whilst I wanted to see if there were patterns of when students got stuck and the strategies they used, it was the case that they would rather just plough on so as to avoid this extra task. Perfect! For some groups of learners it is about creating an expectation that being stuck means you now really have to work and put in some effort. It's nothing to be embarrassed about. But it is a time when you have to dig deep.

12. 'OK, what could you do to help yourself?'

This is merely a prompt for some self-coaching. Students are incredibly creative, thoughtful and, over time, aware of the different strategies that you expect them to use to help their learning when they are stuck. Remind the students of them. And when they repeat your list back to you, invite the students to go and use them!

'Help, I'm stuck' – six progress enhancing alternatives to just giving them the answer

1. **Tweet Elvis (also known as Email God, NASA, Einstein, My Mum ...)**

   This is a lovely technique that will have some students totally bamboozled and others chuckling away at the absurdity of it all. But they will all engage with it. And follow the advice.

   Set up an email address (e.g. God@then.insert.school.email. sch.uk) or a Twitter account (e.g. @I-am-stuck-on-this) and ask students to email or tweet their questions and stuck issues. The recipient could be your teaching assistant, a teaching colleague, the head teacher, a parent helper or a student from another class or year group. All they need to do is offer some guidance back. The amazement when the students get their responses is incredible.

   You could display them on the classroom's projector screen or get all the students logged on to the same Twitter or email account, meaning everyone can benefit from seeing the various sources of help that turn up in the in-tray before either posting the same question or, even worse, asking you for help.

2. **Log on to a vidcasts or podcasts library**

   The Khan Academy (www.khanacademy.org) is fast proving how the learning of many students can benefit from an online video library. You can replicate a personalised version of this by building up a collection of vidcasts and podcasts,

something that could be created by the students themselves (in genuine lazy fashion).

This enables the students to play, pause, rewind and then play back again some of the key points of your explanation. All at their pace and independently of everyone else. It also means that you avoid the situation of having twenty-nine or so students with their learning on hold and their brains in neutral whilst you repeat your explanation to the one student who hasn't yet 'got it'. Which, considering it didn't work the first time, just might fail the second, or the third, or the fourth …

3. **More Progress Coaches**

The use of More Progress Coaches in your class can really help keep progress ticking along in a very lazy way. Having students who can coach others in the strategies of becoming unstuck acts as a motivating force and re-engages students with their learning, as well as being one huge step on from simply having bright students sat next to a slightly less able student, who simply tell their neighbour the answer throughout the lesson.

The success that schools have already had with peer-to-peer schemes, such as peer listeners (involving students of all ages), shows just how capable students are of helping each other without simply giving each other the answers. So, devise a self-certificated coaching course for your More Progress Coaches that explores how they could help other learners when they are stuck.

And, as ever with coaching, the benefits are often two-way. As Module 1 of the training course is likely to be 'What do you do when you are stuck?', even the coaches benefit and increase their stuck repertoire because the group, possibly for the first time, reflect and share their stuck strategies. Hence do not restrict this group to just the so-called 'experts'. It is a perfect opportunity to include someone who is very persistent in using you as a source of help and giving that student the confidence and credibility to lead on the stuck strategies.

If you have a group of students who have never experienced being stuck and are therefore, bereft of strategies there is a simple solution: generate some deliberate stuckness with a puzzles day, for example. They might not like the idea of being stuck and being unable to race to the end of the task, but you will be doing them a massive favour when it comes to making them better learners, as well as giving them greater empathy with others who do get stuck and need time to think of great solutions.

Imagine the collaborative atmosphere in the room when you have the More Progress Coaches weaving their supportive magic throughout the classroom – giving you time to support the bewildered person in the corner,* baffled as to why there is all this outstanding learning going on even though you aren't doing any teaching.

Oh, and whilst you're at it, why not roll this out across the school as it seems selfish to run a programme just for your lessons when it could be easily spread across the school. Especially when it is older More Progress Coaches leading the session for the younger coaches. How lazy is that!

4. Look at the end result

Although this is a cliché, it is nonetheless true that when assembling flat-pack furniture some people will look at the final picture of the instructions and, with the image locked in their mind, set about with great gusto putting together the eighty-seven different pieces without so much as another glance at the booklet. I tried this once and ended up with a door that would only fit when it was hung upside down and a wife who didn't know whether to laugh at me or shout at me and, if both, in which order.

---

*That will be the inspector.

This 'begin with the end in mind' concept is also witnessed in those households where the occupants are on a diet and pin a picture of themselves at their desired shape on the fridge or food cupboard. A subtle reminder of what the process is and what will help them reach the goal.

In the classroom we need a little more than just the end result. After all, if I was trying to teach my son to cycle, just showing him a video or picture of Sir Chris Hoy may not be enough on its own.

So have examples of finished work on display. But rather than just have it as a monument to the current cohort's inadequacies, make sure it is annotated with hints, clues, ideas or examples of specific techniques that were used. I have seen this work well with art, sculptures and equations. A lovely example that sticks in my mind was where a written answer had been broken down into small chunks and then annotated around the outside with progress-prompting questions such as, 'What could you use to find a selection of words to replace *exciting?*'

Whatever the end product, make sure it is not simply there to copy. It is there to prompt the student's own progress, not replicate someone else's.

5. The wall of independence

This is the one-stop shop for independent learners. It is an ever changing, dynamic resource that is invaluable for all learners and that sustains great progress in the lesson. And, in true lazy fashion, you will not have to do a thing. What it boils down to is a wall display on which students write up their questions and others leave answers, suggest definitions, say how they got themselves unstuck, which learning coach helped them, what key facts they have learnt today, which skills they have practised and much more.

On top of that, they can also write up how they managed to sustain progress and what progress they want to make next lesson, thereby turning it into a public declaration of what it takes to help make this progress happen.

On a practical note, my experience tells me that pens benefit from being tethered to the display by a long piece of string and the cheapest way of creating a display is wallpaper lining from a DIY store. In addition, next to their contribution on the display, students will really enjoy writing/signing their name or sticking a picture of their face. In fact, it further adds to the excitement of using the wall. And the more people who use the wall, the better it is.

If you want to offer your class the upgraded version, and create even more engagement, then use liquid chalk pens on glass or cover an item you would not normally write on with Magic Whiteboard paper. There is something about writing on a window, table top, painted wall or door that makes it even more memorable and therefore likely to help the learning remain locked.

6. **3B4ME**

This is one for the student who wants you to think they have tried everything. Quite simply it is your way of insisting that they have tried at least three different strategies (or 4B4ME if you like) before they can come and ask for your help. They should be able to explain how three different independent learning strategies have failed to help them before you offer any assistance.

Hopefully what all this has demonstrated is that being stuck is not the end of the learning process. In fact, it is arguably the beginning. It was an assumption such as this that was behind a head teacher I know asking students at the end of the day how many times they had been stuck that day. If they replied that they hadn't, or that it had only been once or twice, then far from praising the highly differentiated work his staff must have been setting, his conclusion was that the work had been too easy and students were not being challenged enough. He also added a caveat that the students should have a range of strategies to help themselves become unstuck.

I hope too that I have shown you how the stuck student's cry for help and raised hand does not mark the end of your Lazy Teaching approach. Far from it. It signals the time for you to be lazier than ever. What's more, such tough love works. Even with a tomato hunt. I eventually found the elusive Pomodoro di Pachino by resisting the desire to stand in the aisle with my hand up and by doing something different. Namely, tracking down the nearest Waitrose on my smartphone and heading to foreign parts of my home town to buy them, my sense of achievement dulled only by the fact that I had forgotten the Bag for Life. Again. No wonder they last a lifetime!

Chapter 3

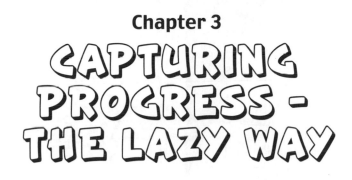

Chapter 3
Capturing Progress –
The Lazy Way

It has been observed that judging progress in a twenty-minute snapshot of a lesson is like watching a three-minute clip of a game of football and predicting the final score. That said, let's assume that all inspectors are highly trained professionals who can smell a good lesson as easily as the Child Catcher can sniff out children in a ball pit. One thing that is guaranteed to ensure the inspector sees your lesson in a good light is if he or she witnesses genuine evidence of progress in that brief window of inspection opportunity. And if you were in need of another reason – can we really have fourteen years of education with no progress? It might just be up to you to make sure that does not happen.

Whether your lessons last all day or for just half an hour, being able to demonstrate progress is what everyone is looking for, so best give them what they want. Not only will it make an inspector happy but as teachers we need to witness the pupils' learning and progress in a lesson so we can help shape what comes next. Simply teaching a scheme of learning is not enough.

So, put your cynicism aside and use these progress-related activities with which you can proverbially slap an inspector over the head; in the same way you would overtly look in your mirrors when taking your driving test or brew fresh coffee when selling your home. If it achieves the desired results – inspectors and learners leave your lesson with big smiles on their faces and you still fulfil the lazy criteria – and no one gets hurt, it's all good.

Lazy Ways to enhance learning and capture progress

1. Going solo

'What have you done for yourself today?' A straightforward question which hopefully generates a long list of responses that highlight independent learning. It is a very simple strategy for making students aware of all the potential they have and to recognise the different sources of help that are available – other than you – as a result of your well-planned lesson.

It is great to see the students keep a list as it acts as a constant reminder that you are the Lazy teacher – and not the learning messiah, who teaches nothing but dependency. And to make sure it is a long list, set a target of at least five things that your learners have done for themselves to enhance learning that day.

If you find the students need some help with this, you could even have some prompts on a 'Please Help Yourself' poster. This, of course, would have been designed by the students for the students. It will simply act as another way of reinforcing all of the ideas that contribute to promoting independent learning.

2. My summary box

At the start of the class students are asked to collect at least five key facts, definitions, formulae, key words or similar over the course of the lesson. These might be overtly communicated by you, or words that they have linked into today's lesson from previous learning. All of the students write/annotate these in a summary box as the lesson progresses.

Occasionally pair up students and ask them to use these summary boxes to form the basis of a reflective learning game such as Pictionary, memory recall or a ranking activity where they have to argue which fact, definition, formulae, etc is the most important. At the end of each learning experience students have a personalised summary of the learning, and they also have the opportunity to link the summary boxes together at the end of topics.

If you want to add a kinaesthetic element to the progress checker, students can move round the room comparing their summary boxes and collecting five additional ideas to place in their box. A whole class summary box works well on a display board or, if space allows, one per group, which is updated as you go along – a bit like 'latest scores' on a football results show.

3. **Daring demonstrations**

Who leads when it comes to giving demonstrations in the class? What would it look and feel like if students took the lead? Now, whilst there may be some health and safety implications to consider, tackling these as opposed to saying, 'I can't let them do it' creates an atmosphere of trust, respect and an overwhelming sense of pride amongst the students that they are responsible for other people's learning. It never fails to engage both the students and the visiting inspector alike when it's Kalid and Gemma leading the class as opposed to you. Likewise, build in opportunities for students to talk about what skills they have been using by setting up mini student demonstrations around the room.

And if you want to eliminate the risk of it going wrong (although learning comes out of every opportunity so don't worry too much), why not film them in advance and build up your own video library of students helping students.

4. **Progress portfolio**

This is basically an essential skills checklist for a subject and offers a way to match the skills and competencies you are promoting across the curriculum. Students then self-assess where they are making progress and get this signed off by other students or adults in the room. The signing-off procedure involves them presenting evidence they have collected themselves or been given by others (e.g. the Progress Paparazzi – see page 28). This might include reviews of their work in a book or folder, contributions to discussions, an e-portfolio, pictures, movies of groupwork – you get the idea that it could be anything.

Furthermore, you can create lots of learning opportunities through the design of the progress portfolios and the use of different diagrams, symbols and images; in fact, it is amazing what the students come up with. I am always curious to see how far removed their ideas are from the bland, seemingly obvious yet overly complicated, levelled statements the profession has decided will be of use. Beyond Ofsted, perhaps the students themselves can move into assessment to help save money and improve effectiveness.

5. Brand spanking new box

For me there is always something about being the first person to read a copy of a newspaper. It just feels better than if you pick up a copy that has already been read. Likewise with learning. Nothing beats something brand spanking new!

This progress checker asks students to identify and record what is genuinely new to them by means of drawing a 'BSN box' in their books and filling it up with all-new material. It is a great way of checking whether you have the pitch of the lesson right. If the boxes remain empty you know you need to throw in some new learning.

You can also extend this into a collaborative activity with a 'BSN wall display' that everyone can see. So much learning can take place simply by visual curiosity. Oh yes, and because you, the teacher, are a learner too, add your spanking new bits on there as well.

6. **Learning speedometer – scream louder for faster learning!**

    Whilst we may all have a fading memory of the Highway Code, we are nonetheless aware that speed limits for different roads are fixed. The beauty of learning is that the speed at which we can (and, indeed, want to) learn is always variable. So rather than rely on the ancient art of guessing how fast to go in a lesson, ask the students to reflect on their contribution to the learning process by plotting their efforts on a learning speedometer.

    The outcome? You understand how fast to structure the learning experience and the students become very aware of what they could be contributing to it.

7. **Progress bar**

    A common feature when we are waiting for a film or software update to download is a progress bar. It shows you how far you have progressed. Likewise, the totaliser showing how much money has been made for the new church roof (which is now a thankless task since the price of copper and lead has gone, well, through the roof).

    At the start of the lesson, ask students to draw a bar or totaliser in their books/files and divide it up into five sections so that each bar represents 20% (which obviously provides a glorious opportunity to slip in some numeracy – although try not to giggle at this point during an observation as it is a bit of a giveaway that such support of the maths department is not commonplace).

    Then ask the students what they think would represent the different stages of progress towards the final outcome. It might mean that the 20% completion target is to have 'read all the resources', the 40% target is to have 'decided which resources are of the most use' and so on. It is a simple way for the students to create their own road map, keep an eye on time and make sure that those who like to see each little step

are as happy as those who like to see the big picture of everything that needs to be done.

When it is under way, ask the students not only to track their own progress – noting when they completed the different stages (useful for you in terms of correlating how long you thought a task would take and how long it actually did take) – but also to provide a running commentary to you in writing or verbally about each stage, identifying how easy or difficult each one was.

Just a note of caution for the first time you use it: those who like colouring in tend to shade up to 80% instantly, to keep you off their back, before then crashing on the last stage and needing a boost to start all over again. I call them my Windows kids.

8. Tweenaries

The name stems from the technique used on Twitter, but the idea works equally well using paper and pens as it does in an ICT-rich learning environment. For this to work you need your class divided into teams, with each team headed up by a Learning Champion (that is to say, the students you have nominated to lead the various different teams you have operating in your classroom). If you are new to the idea of dividing your class into teams, it will be a revelation. It won't take you long to discover most things can be presented as a challenge if you have such teams, even finding a missing glue stick lid! And, as with any well managed team, make sure you rotate roles. So rotate the post of Learning Champion within each team depending on the task or challenge in front of the class. It is after all, yet another, lazy, way of personalising your planning for the class. Then simply follow the steps below:

- ■ Teacher sets question to class.

- ■ Class tweets, emails or passes pieces of paper with their answers on to the Learning Champion.

- Learning Champion decides the best answer, states why and passes this to the teacher.

- Learning Champion returns unused answers with feedback to the team.

- Teacher tweets/sends best answers to the class.

- Everyone carries on.

Or to offer choice (and we know how important that is) here it is as a diagram:

I saw this work very effectively in an enterprise lesson when a teacher was modelling real-life work situations and, for fully justified reasons, kept interrupting the flow of the group with a tweenary. It was interesting how the group soon learnt to deal with these in a matter of seconds and not to be distracted from their main task – just proving that checking progress does not need to be accompanied by a massive handbrake on the learning.

9. A4-ull day of progress – A4-ull week of progress

Imagine you had to fill a piece of A4 paper for your progress portfolio (see 4 above) with what it is you have learnt and discovered today. It might consist of facts, drawings, key words, thoughts, questions, symbols or all of the above. It would act as an incredibly powerful reflection tool to be used both within twenty-four hours to help lock in the learning, as well as at the end of the week to help recall and make permanent the students' understanding of the skills and knowledge they have acquired.

If you are feeling particularly brave, you could post them on the school website or use community noticeboards or other places where you can display information. Or, if you are lucky enough to have volunteers working in the school, it is a great activity for them to discuss their A4-ull sheets with the students.

Decisions on this task will vary depending on how far you want the reflection and recall to spread. Is it just one subject or the whole curriculum? Just for your work or can colleagues contribute as well? Is it simply for use in school or can its application extend beyond the school day? After all, progress won't happen just in school.

10. Must–should–could

Nothing new about this one, as it is often seen at the start of a lesson for differentiating aims and/or outcomes. That said, I have always had my doubts about must-should–could as a lesson starter. Put yourself in the shoes of the learner for whom there is little incentive for them to aim high. 'You could do this, maybe' is hardly a ringing example of are-you-up-for-it, motivational tub-thumping! Many teachers will be thinking, 'Totally essential–compulsory–optional. But if you want to leave on time ...'

Yet towards the end of a lesson during which they may not have zipped along as you would have wished (especially if

Ofsted Rapide are in residence with one of their twenty-minute observations) it can become useful to grab a small period of time to maximise the progress. So, instead of going all red-necked and clammy, spend a minute on a quick must–should–could exercise, making sure you ram home the 'must' element with everything you want done. After a mini protest, watch the atmosphere totally change in the room.

Far better to stop and execute this three-worded progress resuscitation package than to plough on regardless to the lesson's limp end; whereupon other than getting through it, other outcomes will be non-existent. Indeed, when you think about it, there is nothing lazy about teaching a lesson that will have to be done all over again because although you might have taught it, they didn't learn it.

11. That links to ...

To make the most out of our teaching and their learning, we need to capture progress that extends beyond any one subject we happen to be teaching. Every now and then we need to take a helicopter view so students make links not only within and across topics but also across the whole curriculum. It is also a way of nurturing your lazy ethos just that little bit more; you never know, a colleague may well have taught the students some of this topic before.

A new bit of learning in science may have a link to design technology or PE. Likewise, understanding a process in geography might help them – or indeed inspire them – in art. Simply ask, 'As a result of knowing this, what can you link it to inside and outside of this subject?' and see what happens. If we don't ask the question, they never have the opportunity to think in this important way.

And if you want a point-scoring system for 'That links to ...', it's the same formula as *A Question of Sport*'s 'Home and Away' round – one point for a link to your subject; two points for an all-important cross-curricular link.

12. Where could we go next?

Ensuring learners have ownership of their learning – for example, by offering a choice of tasks, assessments or topics – is well documented in both formal and informal research as a sure-fire way of improving levels of engagement. What is more, helping students see a 'big picture' of the topic they are studying significantly helps them to understand where they are, where they've been and where they are going; which also helps with their motivation and learning. This may be as simple (although not very powerful) as a list of topics and key words, or as exciting (and much more effective) as an infographic of questions, facts, diagrams and topics.

Combine this 'big picture' idea with allowing students choice over their direction and you can really start to see them race ahead with their learning. 'Where could we go next?' simply asks them to plot their next move based on what they are currently learning. Not only do they then take ownership *and* often find out the answers before you have to teach them, but they also plan their own route of their own understanding. Who said learning had to be linear? And who decreed that topics would be taught in the order they currently are? That order might suit you, but does it suit the learners?

13. What have we dropped?

This flips progress checking on its head. Constantly saying what you have achieved can become quite sterile and robotic. By flipping the question around and asking, 'What have you *not* done?', you not only surprise the students, but the mild sense of paranoia you induce prompts a close scrutiny of the success criteria and a natural tendency to refocus. You can also hear a quiet sense of appreciation from your class as they think, 'Nice twist, Miss!'

14. Silent squiggles/mute masterpieces

A great one for those moments when you have an end-of-week headache, or you want to work on learning skills or it is *that* class again and you need to totally outfox them with an idea which appears easy but is, in fact, really challenging.

The activity involves giving pairs or groups of students an opportunity to debate a key question that is posed by you or, even better in a Lazy Way, one of the students. The twist is that it is a silent debate. To do this they might have to draw or write their responses but, to turn the learning knife even further, you will be limiting their use of words and insisting they use symbols or diagrams as appropriate.

Another version is that they mime or act out their point of view, which is an ideal opportunity to recognise that drama is not just a subject done by English teachers but, for many students, a really useful way of locking in the learning.

When you use this technique, make sure you do not fall into the trap of everyone watching everyone. Drama in the classroom is not about giving performances. Consider how you could divide up the class so you have clusters of students miming and drawing to each other, rather than one group at a time. If there is something that warrants a whole-class showcase, make sure it is adding something to the learning process, such as modelling effective learning skills, as it is very easy to kill progress with a string of performances without a purpose.

15. How do you feel?

This is one of my favourite progress diagrams. You can spend hours looking at it and reflecting on how you feel now, and also looking back and remembering how you have felt at different stages in the past. And because it is engaging, it presents you with an ideal opportunity to prompt a dialogue about learning as students explain their responses to questions such as:

- Where are you on the emotions tree?

- What would represent a better position for you?

- Now we have tried that harder question, where are you?

- What is going to stop you falling out the tree?

In my book, this is something a great deal more emotionally intelligent and useful for both the learner and the teacher than holding up bits of red, amber or green card.

16. Souvenir hunting

If you see a play at the theatre, a concert at a stadium or even a local am-dram production, it is likely that not only will you be offered a souvenir but you will buy one, even if it is mainly full of adverts for taxi companies or local independent investment consultants you used to teach and who failed their maths GCSE at least twice that you know of.

And why do we buy one (apart from knowing that should you ever cross that inspector again, you have evidence to prove the student clearly did make progress in the maths lesson, he just hid it very well)? So we can remember the experience of the performance. The sights, the sounds, the feelings and, hopefully, the joy it brought you. If souvenirs work for that local attempt at *The Pirates of Penzance*, then maybe they could work for learning too.

Every day, thousands of amazing learning experiences are created for students. The vast majority of those are gone forever, never to be repeated or benefited from again. What if the students used the 'souvenir effect' to capture the learning for use later on?

To follow the lead from the theatre, they could break down the learning into a series of 'acts' to making a running order of their learning, write biographies for the main characters, sketch out the key technical requirements for the 'performance', record a series of songs for a CD or design logos to form a set of postcards that transform into revision cards. And that's before you have let them loose with audio and video recording devices. After all, there may be an occasion when they need to watch the whole performance again. And no one is a fan of unpaid matinees in any industry.

Not only do they have to be on top of their game in the lesson, perhaps recording pieces to camera or writing a script for making a podcast, but they are also creating a long-lasting resource that might negate the need for running extra catch-up and booster revision sessions later in the term. The student's souvenir effectively offers an 'anytime, anywhere' personalised review and revision session – if you had asked them to make one.

17. Hold the front page!

This is a really effective progress checker with a lovely literacy twist running through it. Students are asked to summarise their learning in the form of a headline for a newspaper, magazine or newsletter. Not only will the headline change as the learning progresses, but playing with different publications for which they are writing the headline adds that extra frisson!

For one added newsroom-esque challenge, add in a deadline element to get them working at pace. And if you want to really crank up the pressure, select different numbers of words that must be in the headline; anything between one and ten does the trick in my experience.

18. One word

This is one of those activities that falls perfectly into the low access–high challenge strategy so beloved of Lazy teachers everywhere. Ask students to write down single words on a blank piece of paper at various intervals in the lesson or during the analysis of a resource such as a film. The single words should best reflect what they are learning – be it a new term, connection, thought or feeling. Make sure they spread the words out over the whole sheet with plenty of space between each word because you then have more options to play, sorry *progress*, with them later (both in the current and subsequent lessons – learning is never neatly formed into lesson-long lengths of time, is it?).

It is worth noting that, on the surface, choosing a single word to describe your new learning periodically during the lesson seems quite simple. Yet it is actually quite a tricky thing to do, so if you are feeling kind you can always offer a little slack and give them a two-word option.

What you are building, as the lesson progresses, is a personalised 'word bank' that you can then go on to use in a series of even more challenging activities, such as:

- Classifying words into groups, with students choosing the headings.

- Choosing any seven words and writing a short paragraph that includes all those words, and that also links to your learning today.

- Identifying the longest/shortest sentence you can make using as many of the words as possible.

- Writing exam questions that link to today's topic, where your words would be in the answers.

- Using as many of the words as possible to create a 'link and think map'. This involves students starting on one word on their sheet of words, choosing another and linking them together. This process then continues and becomes a sort of word association game, based on the words they have selected to reflect their own learning.

For example, in a history lesson where students are summarising a film clip in a number of single words, they might subsequently show how '*armoury* links to *fatigue* in soldiers but not in higher ranking *officers* who had *horses'*. It would have been difficult to record this in its entirety during the film (let alone think of higher order connections). Usually, merely writing down the key points, the typical instruction, results in an undercurrent of groans and murmurings of 'What did they say?' and 'Can I see what you have written?' as the film reaches a dramatic climax.

19. Build your own quiz

This is one of the laziest ways of capturing progress, as not only does this deliver for you in this lesson, it also delivers for you in the next. And possibly even the one after that, as it offers material to start, end and break up a long lesson, as well as for homework tasks.

Simply ask the students to write down question-and-answer couplets throughout the lesson, with questions on one side of the paper and answers on the back. If you don't trust the class with this method, then ask them to record questions and answers separately, but get them to write their names on the papers (or code them) so you know who to see to match up the questions and answers.

You can then rotate questions amongst the students in class, set them for homework, use them as killer questions (the very hardest and most difficult of the questions – after all making progress may at times mean getting stuck!) or as 'hot seating' material. Very simple. Very lazy. And actually very clever, as sometimes we put great emphasis on writing answers but very little on the formulation of questions. Furthermore, it generates a real sense of pride that their work is being used for other people's benefit because, when you think about it, that doesn't happen very often.

20. Biggest–best–beautiful

This activity owes its origin to some students I was working with for a one-off lesson. We began discussing what was the best book – and not because we had been asked to because it was Book Week (which the rate of technological development may just determine has a whole new meaning within a matter of years).

As the debate rumbled on, I was amazed at how articulate the students were in their appraisal of different texts. One of them said, 'Even if it is the best, it is not the biggest selling'; closely followed by another dissenting, but more gentle, voice that added, 'Nor is it the most beautiful book'.

And from that literary debate, biggest–best–beautiful was born. And it seems to work in lots of different contexts. Which is the biggest, best, most beautiful part of our body? Piece of music? Colour? Painting? Drink? Chemical reaction? I have used it as a way of showing how students' thinking has progressed, changed and altered as a result of being shown and considering a number of resources shared over the lesson.

For example, if you were looking at bridges, how can you determine the biggest, best, most beautiful bridge? You might share pictures, statistics and facts to determine an answer. But is that a definitive answer? Did you mean longest-biggest (Danyang–Kunshan Grand Bridge, China) or highest-biggest (Si Du River Bridge, China)? Is it the same for an ant? The more you think, the more challenging it becomes. Progress is clearly shown because evidence is sourced to back up opinions in what, I warn you, could become a heated debate! And that's before you start on best and beautiful.

21. Thinking hexagons

As soon as I was introduced to hexagonal learning by The Learning Spy* (aka David Didau, a head of English who has worked wonders on attainment in, and enjoyment of, his subject by focusing on genuine learning experiences), I was taken both by its simplicity and its effectiveness.

Where possible, ask the students to draw and cut out ten hexagons (or, if you need to save time or brain space, provide them with a pre-drawn sheet to cut out or the hexagons themselves if you have some keen cutter-outters looking to gain a few 'well done' points).

As the lesson progresses, individuals or groups add a key word to each hexagon. As soon as you can make a connection, you align the hexagons so anywhere they touch there is a connection which they can clearly explain. A variety of different patterns can be made, with the ultimate goal to see how many sides of each hexagon you can get to touch. Patterns change.

---

*See http://learningspy.co.uk/2012/01/28/hexagonal-learning/.

Words are crossed out and replaced with new words. New connections are made. There's a real buzz and some great learning.

You can even ask the class to take photos of how their model has evolved and get them to turn it into a time-lapse movie or just work with their final creations; a real favourite of mine and the students I've used it with. And so we don't let these photos fall into the category of 'firework learning' (i.e. a lot of effort but all over after a single use), you could edit and use them as a basis for lots of other thinking games. For example:

■ Project the image of a completed hexagon pattern that has some of the words blanked out and see how many different words would fit in the gap.

■ Project the image of a completed hexagon pattern leaving just the first letter of each word for students to recall and make the connections.

■ Project the image of a completed hexagon pattern on which the students have to write a question – the answer to which will be one of the words from the hexagon pattern.

And at this point those of a certain age and TV watching habits are already ahead of me in thinking we could use these questions to play the legendary quiz show *Blockbusters*, as students move from one side of the pattern to the other (and, of course, get to say the infamous line, 'Can I have a "P" please Bob?').

As the students' skills develop, or as a means of differentiation, you can apply the same principle using different shapes so there are less or more connecting sides, or mix and match shapes to make it like a crazy paving thinking and connections game!

22. Talking triads

It is so tempting to utter the phrase, 'Turn to your partner and discuss three new things you have learnt today' and half sit back, knowing you have ticked the 'peer assessment' and 'checking of progress' boxes. But the very fact that you only allow yourself to half sit back suggests that, deep down, you know there is another, better, more Lazy Way of doing things; one that offers an opportunity to work on not one but three different skills as well as assessing learning progress. And talking triads is it.

To do this, simply place students into groups of three, using yourself and a teaching assistant – if you are still lucky enough to have one – when needed. Roles are then allocated for the triad:

■ Speaker – explains the topic, the progress they have made or expresses their opinion on a particular issue.

■ Questioner – listens carefully, asks for clarification or for
further detail before posing questions back that reflect
the fact that (a) they have listened and (b) can offer a
challenge back, which of course helps with their own
learning.

■ Assessor – observes the process and provides feedback to
both speaker and questioner and can, where appropriate,
make links to the success criteria or levels when you are
using them.

So when you are feeling lazy in the wrong sense of the word
and are about to say, 'Turn to your partner', remember, as the
song goes, 'Three is a magic number'.

23. Leave with a question

How many times a day are you asked questions that are
directly connected with learning? I mean *really* probing questions that give an insight into the progress and links the
learners are making for themselves? Perhaps more in the primary phase than the secondary (oh, that statement will
generate a few letters!) but still not enough for my liking. And
certainly not enough to offset the plethora of 'Is this right?' or
'What do I do next?' type questions. Yet we know that asking
the right questions often offers more insight into the progress
being made than simply answering another question. This
activity addresses this current imbalance as well as, quite
rightly, linking together some of the curriculum work on
questioning.

During, or at the end of the lesson, students write a question
on a sticky note or piece of paper. The question could be
something that they still need answering to help them with
the outcome(s), something they have become curious about as
a result of the lesson or something they think is a way of
showing what they have learnt but others may have missed.

These questions then, by means of a gratifying slap, get posted
onto your question wall – which could be a sheet of paper that

you pin up each time you see the class, ready for use later in the lesson (or at the start of the next lesson if the gratifying slap is part of the exit routine!).

When the right learning opportunity arises, students can grab a question (not their own) with which to complete the second part of the process – answering the question. And merely having a question to answer can in turn lead to loads more individual and collaborative learning experiences and yes, you have guessed it, more progress.

Depending on your ethics, you could of course slip a few of your own questions onto the question wall, including some carefully selected ones to emphasise key points you may have axed because your slot in the lesson was up and it was time for the students to get busy.

And what about those questions the students can't answer? Put them back on the question wall and see how long it takes someone to come up with an answer. It won't be long, especially if you bill them as 'Impossible Questions That No one Can Answer'. For some it would appear that there is nothing more satisfying than picking up the learning gauntlet and throwing it back in the teacher's face. Still, if that's what it takes for progress, so be it. I have sacrificed much more. The grey hairs tell me that.

P.S. Always invite any visitor to the room to try and answer one – including those who have only got twenty minutes to spare!

24. Stretch it – bank it

This is a simple way of showing progress and looking at detail, which you could link to the quizzes that many of our students will be taking in one form or another during the year. OK, exams and tests; but again, as with lesson observations, we can do much to alter how we feel by how we talk about them.

This idea is loosely based on the game where you write a story collaboratively but you fold over the paper after you have written your bit to make it both absurd and funny. The twist in this activity is that you don't fold the paper over, thus rendering it less absurd; although, if you do have a go from time to time with folding the paper over, it is a very funny game.

Offer the group a sentence such as 'The First World War started in 1914' or 'Julius Caesar was a Roman general'. The paper is then passed on and the next person has to add something to the list and, importantly, initial it. This ever-growing, collaborative snapshot weaves its way around the class before going back to you or whoever wrote the original sentence. And just like Pass the Parcel seemed to be the most boring party game in the world if the parcel was not within two people of arriving with you, there is no need to limit the roving statement to just one.

If the piece of paper arrives at a student who feels he or she has nothing to add, ensure they (a) make sure there is nothing on the paper that they don't already know – if there is they write it down and (b) start a new thread, because just because they did not know about this subject does not mean they can't share something else they may have learnt.

This activity also helps build great respect and collaboration in the group, enabling you to showcase some highly effective behaviours for learning. And, of course, you'll note that the Lazy teacher is again, ahem, suitably sidelined by this exercise. I thank you!

25. Thirty seconds to tell me ...

It is a much-touted notion that if you can't pitch your business idea within the duration of an elevator ride you still have work to do on your product and its marketing. It is an idea known to our friends across the Pond as the 'elevator pitch', something that has a much better ring to it than the UK version, the 'lift pitch', which sounds like something you do when you cheat in golf. As a Lazy Progress activity, though, it is a great idea to use. If a student can't tell you what progress they have made this lesson in their thirty-second slot they will have to ... well, I will leave that up to you.

This strategy sees them gathering all sorts of work, thoughts and evidence which, when presented with wild gesticulations of the arms, a slightly frantic voice and pathetically pleading looks, could be just the progress checker you need to offer choice and freedom as well as show your deeply caring and sensitive side.

26. Success Spies

One sure way to maximise the amount of progress you capture in the lesson is to ensure you welcome progress that is not necessarily linked exclusively to your outcomes. If you just restrict progress to the probably single, teacher-led, didactic outcome that you scrawl up on the board at the first sight of the inspector, then none of you will receive the full praise you deserve.

In any lesson, learning is never restricted to what you decree are the learning outcomes. So much more will have happened that you will miss – you just need some extra eyes and ears to help you. Which is where your Success Spies come in.

Whereas the Progress Paparazzi (see page 28) are overt and students may be putting on a show for them, the spies are covert, undertaking pre-published or secret missions. Either way the aim of the Success Spies is to capture the wonderful unsung work of those who might not normally attract the attention of the teacher. They snoop, they sneak about, they pry, they watch and learn and they feed back, like the big snitches they are, to the rest of the class on anything from the skills they have seen and the attitudes they have witnessed to the knowledge they have noticed people acquiring or the behaviours they have witnessed that made for great learning.

Creating a climate in which learners actually want to be spied on, and wallow smugly in the positive feedback, is a real way of binding together a group and having some fun in the process. It is an approach that works equally well in groups as it does across a whole class. Do it well and your students will soon want to be the ones who are secretly kept behind at the end of the lesson, for that will surely mean a secret mission is coming up …

Hopefully over the last few pages you will have spotted that all these approaches to capturing progress have two common elements:

1. It is the students who are capturing the progress.

2. At no point is the learning coming to a shuddering halt in order to capture progress.

You may also begin to detect that capturing progress is not just for school inspectors. It is part of setting up engaging learning experiences. The two go hand in hand. Like lazy and outstanding.

The most common concern articulated to me when I work with teachers around the country is, 'How can I squeeze this and everything else into the lesson?' And I deliberately use the word 'squeeze' as that is the one most commonly used. My response is always that if you are simply shoehorning it in, on top of everything else, to make the lesson more tightly packed than before, then you are right to think it won't work. Adding more to try and get more has never been the Lazy Way.

Capturing progress happens naturally when lessons are structured with the Lazy Way in mind. Students will learn more when you teach less. Similarly, students will progress more when you check less. Leave that to them, for that is the Lazy Way.

Chapter 4

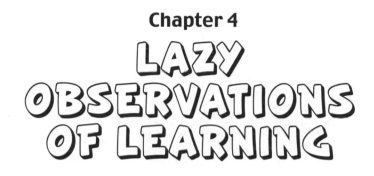

LAZY OBSERVATIONS OF LEARNING

Chapter 4
Lazy Observations
of Learning

It's a long shot born out of desperation and, yes, fear. And it never works. The idea is that if I persuade the dentist to like me, through my natural charm and wit, then he will simply give my teeth a cursory going over before declaring me good to go and offering me an appointment for twelve months time in order to conduct the ritual all over again. If I really push the boat out and turn on the sort of linguistic charm normally reserved for new parents and local journalists, I live in hope that he may just send me happily on my way without even putting me in the chair. But, like I say, as a strategy it never works. My other option of not turning up would. But such is my paranoia about falling below 85% attendance and getting a letter from the attendance officer and a court summons, I can't contemplate that. So instead I am left with the talking-my-way-out-of-it option.

Like many people, I tend to talk excessively when I am nervous. Excessively and quickly. And sweatily. Which means anything could come out as long as something comes out. And if something is coming out then at least we can avoid that state for which so many teachers seem to have a passionate aversion. Silence.

And I don't mean children being silent; that's fine. It is the teacher being silent that is the challenge. Just take a timer into the classroom and allow yourself no more than ten minutes of teacher talk in any hour. You will be making all sorts of accusations about damp getting into the timer before you realise what is really at fault.

For many teachers, the equivalent to my dentist visits is lesson observations – although, to be fair, you don't get an anaesthetic on the way in or a lollipop on the way out. Having another adult in the room, whose purpose is to make some sort of judgement on you at a professional level, has a nasty habit of making people panic. I mean really panic. And, if that adult happens to be an inspector, really, *really* panic. And, just like my dental appointments, this panic leads to you talking excessively, even though you know that this is the worst thing you can do under an Ofsted framework in which it is quite clearly stated that too much teacher talk means you will never reach the giddy heights of 'outstanding', no matter how erudite your words of wisdom.

It is somewhat ironic, therefore, that the laziest way to get through your lesson observation is by talking. The key is not to talk *at the students*, but *with the observer*. If you are being observed in a lesson, be prepared to add 'have a conversation with the observer' to your list of 'thou shalts'.

The Lazy Observation of Learning (LOL – which for those of you up on your text speak is something you might well *not* be doing when you get told you are being observed) means teachers and observers have several conversations *during* the lesson; not after the lesson, not five minutes three days later squeezed in over lunch, but a decent conversation slap bang in the middle of the lesson. Because if you can't manage that, then you are working too hard. Which means, of course, that the students aren't. So, with that in mind, if you're being observed for the whole lesson of, say, an hour, then you should aim to have not one but three such conversations, which, oddly enough, works out at one per twenty minutes. Funny how some things work out. LOL!

Now, once you have stopped laughing, the inevitable question of, 'How can I possibly find the time to do that as well as meet the needs of all the learners, have a starter and a plenary, check progress, take the register, fill in the report cards and squeeze in some literacy and numeracy, let alone create a cultural, moral and religious subplot to the learning?' has probably popped into your head. But remember: you are a Lazy teacher.

The whole point of the Lazy Way, and all the strategies that go with it, is that they genuinely free you up from teaching. And as we reduce the amount of time we spend actually teaching, not only can we start observing the learning more but also use the time for other things, such as having a chat with an observer. Not in a nervous way, but because why would you want anyone who visits your learning environment to miss out on understanding the rationale behind your approach to your teaching and their learning?

To avoid the gibberish that may flow when you are talking to someone wielding a clipboard, let's move our story from the dentist to the restaurant if we may. Below I have designed a three-course 'table d'hôte' menu with a series of questions for each stage of any lesson to whet your appetite for how to guide your in-lesson conversations. Summarised in their simplest form, they enable you, the teacher, to articulate your intended lesson, clarify what progress might look and sound like, as well as review how the lesson is going and what changes you might make as you go along.

For the observer, they enable him or her to clarify the pedagogical approaches being applied, hear how the needs of all learners are being met and gauge the teacher's understanding of what is happening in front of them; all of which adds up to making the judgement process a lot easier. Or, dare I suggest it, lazier.

The observation question menus are written from the observer's point of view, purely because it is more often than not the observer who is the one formulating and asking questions. However, for the teacher they act as a summary of the questions we should be able to answer about the learning; the answers to which will give the observer a real insight into the professional thinking that has gone into the lesson.

The key aspect to using them in your lesson observations is that it forces you to be lazy, to take a step back and to observe what is happening. I cannot think of one lesson where, if you have independent learning at the forefront of your intentions, Lazy Lesson observation conversations will not be able to take place. What you end up with is high quality learning conversations that showcase planning, professional thinking and independent learning, as well as cutting down teacher talk and, well, nervous prattle.

Maybe I should work on a set to use at the dentist.

Lazy observation questions – starters

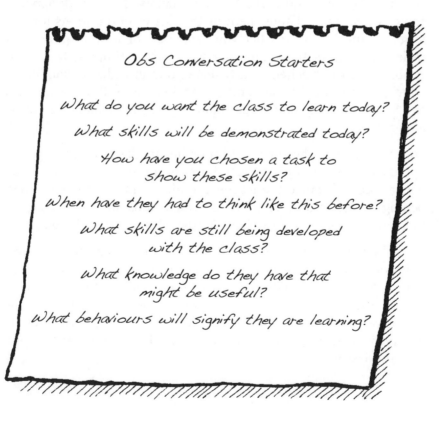

Obs Conversation Starters

What do you want the class to learn today?

What skills will be demonstrated today?

How have you chosen a task to show these skills?

When have they had to think like this before?

What skills are still being developed with the class?

What knowledge do they have that might be useful?

What behaviours will signify they are learning?

If we take the learning experience to be an hour, then within the first few minutes (and if you want to push me on that I mean within the first three minutes) the observer and the teacher should be able to have a conversation based around these questions. The technique does not involve asking or answering all of these questions. Rather, they are there to act as a stimulus for a discussion about what learning is going to happen, why it has been planned in this particular way and what measures are in place to show progress is being made as a result of it. And the very fact that a conversation can take place within the first three minutes means there is every chance that the class is up and running with their independent learning from the very start. Perfect Lazy Progress from the off!

What's more, it is also an opportunity to talk data. After all, as Gareth Beynon quite rightly says, 'Data starts a conversation' (although if you are at a dinner party, it also ends one). So when better than at the start of the lesson where it can act as the scaffolding around which you start your conversation about individual students, how they learn, what you are doing to make sure it happens and what you will do if it doesn't look like it is. Or in other words, neatly arranged as an equation:

Data + Observation = Action

Now the quick witted amongst you will have spotted the immediate opportunity to turn that into the acronym DOA or Dead On Arrival, which is how many of us feel when turning up to a twilight INSET, especially if it is on a topic such as data. However, turn it to real use, as this equation helps you to, and it will be time well spent.

Data

What summative information have you got on the student in terms of progress, attainment, CAT scores, target grades, entry levels and the like? In addition, what else do you know that could have an impact on learning, such as special educational needs and disabilities information or maybe even their hopes, dreams and ambitions?

Observation

Whilst indulging in some Lazy Teaching, what have you observed about the students' learning behaviours? This is where you get the opportunity to really demonstrate that professional acuity which shows you don't just teach subjects – you teach children. What is it that you notice about each individual in your class? Are they reluctant to take the lead? Are they overly assertive? Do they respond well to private praise? Are they divergent thinkers? The list could go on ...

And finally, the most important bit which is often overlooked in all the reams of data that gets printed about each class:

Action

What are *you* doing about it? How does your planning reflect the data and what you have observed about the learning behaviours of the individuals in your class? It might be that you engineer it so that an able but over-confident thinker in the class, who lacks reflection skills and is prone to shouting out the (often wrong) answer, is forced by your careful planning to have a listening role. Or an underperforming student, according to the data, who is seemingly lacking self-esteem is placed in a group of very respect-ful individuals and promoted to be team leader.

And since having the specific needs of all thirty students on the boil at once might prove too much, and be in danger of becoming personalised learning gone wrong, my suggestion would be to choose five students to focus on each term. Not only do they then get some genuine and effective personalisation, but you also have an opportunity to focus on them when you are observing the group to make sure your actions still match the observations and the data. Besides, data is one of things that hopefully isn't for life; it is just until the next assessment comes along. Which is likely to be way before Christmas.

Lazy observation questions – mains

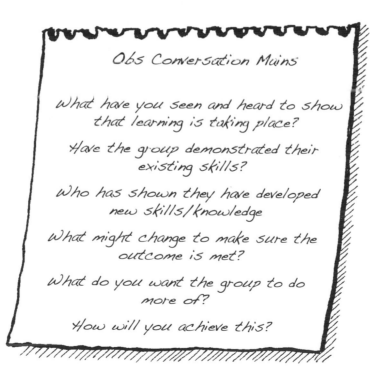

Obs Conversation Mains

What have you seen and heard to show that learning is taking place?

Have the group demonstrated their existing skills?

Who has shown they have developed new skills/knowledge

What might change to make sure the outcome is met?

What do you want the group to do more of?

How will you achieve this?

During the mains of our independent learning feast – which as a rule should last around three quarters of the lesson, with every minute more being better still – you will have another opportunity to have a conversation with the observer. This time the theme is twofold: (1) What has gone on in the lesson so far and how effective has it been for the learners? (2) Where has progress been made and how engaged are they?

Despite the best lesson planning in the world, an activity that looks good on paper may have been met with universal disapproval or lethargy – especially with the mood-altering presence of an inspector in the room. To sum it up nicely, you may wish to use a phrase from the thought-provoking Dr Barry Hymer, who suggests teachers ask, 'What's the ASDA verdict' where ASDA means: Are Students Dormant or Active?

These thoughts link into the questions above and offer you an opportunity to demonstrate something which might ordinarily happen but under the pressure of the observation may be lost: your ability to react to the learning in front of you and show that, because you have time to observe, you don't miss opportunities to clarify or extend opportunities for progress in learning.

As a result of this conversation, and following our DOA principle, you now have permission (not that that it was really ever needed in the first place) to divorce yourself from your original lesson plan, take note of the observer's feedback and your own observations – 'I knew they wouldn't respond to a colleague's lesson plan; should of just gone with what works' – and action some changes – 'Let's just use what I know works'.

And when you exercise that permission, both you and the learners will be well rewarded (and any observer worth their salt will be suitably impressed).

Lazy observation questions – desserts

Obs Conversation Desserts

What skills/knowledge have the group learnt?

In what part of the lesson did the most significant learning take place?

What did you learn today about the group that you didn't know before?

How will you apply what you have learnt in planning the next lesson?

How do you feel about the lesson?

The last series of questions that takes place in our Lazy Lesson observation repast once again has many benefits and is crucial both to this lesson and its feedback as well as impacting on the success of the next.

The main theme of this course is to highlight the effective behaviours that you witnessed, to identify which groups made the most progress and also to describe how you personally felt about the lesson. This is something that is often overlooked, and that is a shame as a characteristic of many, if not all, outstanding lessons is that both the teacher and the students speak enthusiastically about their time together. So, like a nervous chef who has just managed to bake the perfect soufflé without it deflating during the judging section of *Ready, Steady, Cook,* smile, breathe and give the impression that you, as well as the students, really enjoyed the lesson. Besides, it is almost over, bar the judging ...

Lazy Observation of Learning feedback

With the conversations and observation over, there are still further benefits to the Lazy Observation of Learning process. Namely, in the post-observation feedback session both observer and observed will genuinely feel that teaching and learning will improve in the future. The observation has been for the purpose of improving student learning and not for collating a secret database or completing a self-evaluation form (leave the purely summative observations for when Ofsted Rapide arrive as they will not be hanging around for post-observation formative discussions).

As a result of knowing that the feedback session will result in progress, the stress that sometimes accompanies post-observation feedback (come on, we have all looked at our observer and thought, 'I would like to see you have a go with that class') is much reduced, because why wouldn't we want our own teaching and learning to progress? Just like the students.

The feedback process can start with a dialogue structured around a few What Went Wells (WWWs) and Even Better Ifs (EBIs), taking into account the different parts of the lesson. This is far better than the observer conducting a linear trawl through the lesson and missing the pedagogical context to prior or future activities. We are a fairly reflective bunch, and for someone to list what it was you were doing in the seventeenth minute merely highlights that you have another forty-three minutes of descriptive feedback to come. What's more, if you are receiving the feedback, you can instantly begin to articulate how you could use your WWWs and EBIs in future lessons. It is good to use them promptly, and it is even better for the observer to hear how you have contextualised the points and want to go on and use them.

Another benefit is that having already discussed key observation topics, such as progress and student outcomes, throughout the three conversations in the lesson, there is already a subliminal agreement with your observer with regard to the lesson grade you will receive. It would take a pretty poor observer to sit through the entire lesson and then whip an unsatisfactory grade out of his or her, er, hat as a matter of complete surprise. The conversations that form the bedrock of the Lazy Observation of Learning are there to be used as an in-lesson coaching tool, as well as assisting in making judgements. There is (or should be) no fun in sitting back and watching an unsatisfactory lesson roll out in front of you.

Finally, because you have had an on-going dialogue during the lesson, the formal feedback is a lot quicker, meaning you can grab the opportunity to spend more time talking to your observer about your wider professional development. And bearing in mind the observer is most likely to be your line manager, senior leader or even your head teacher, that's some valuable 'me-time' to grab. Done well, it will be a conversation that not only benefits your learners but also you (especially useful when the internal promotion is on the menu).

Lazy Observations of Learning – a whole school perspective

Hopefully you are picking up that the lesson observation process can become a really powerful tool for improving the progress of everyone in the school. So, once you have conquered your fears and learnt to talk about the learning *whilst being observed*, and seen how it works, you will then be in a very strong position to spread the word, engaging more reluctant colleagues and promoting Lazy Observations of Learning with them. And let them laugh out loud in the first instance as well. Who knows, you may even sell them on the entire Lazy Way! Of course, there will always be recalcitrants and recidivists, so what follows now is another raft of game-changing Lazy Way strategies to help sway the undecided and get them to engage with the whole concept of 'progress'.

These tactics will certainly help your colleagues avoid that at-the-dentist gabble from which so many of them will suffer too. And if they suffer from it, so will their students.

Five ways to engage others with the Lazy Observations of Learning

1. **Let them come and see you have a live Lazy Lesson observation**

    If seeing is believing, then invite a colleague in for a triple whammy of professional development as they watch the students, you and the observer in action. We might pop into colleagues' lessons quite often but rarely do we pay a visit during a high-stakes one, preferring instead to shepherd people away whispering, 'Don't go in there, they're having an observation', as if we were ushering people past the site of a colonic irrigation. This hardly promotes the process as a public, pain-free, personally enriching and developmental process (an observation, that is, not a colonic irrigation). Yet an observation is fertile continuing professional development (CPD) ground. Inviting in colleagues will also help instantly answer their questions or fears – being a Lazy teacher you can answer them on the spot as you go along.

2. **Design and share the paperwork with your colleagues**

    There is no single perfect lesson observation pro forma that you have to or should use for observations, although I do prefer one that contains a mixture of open space for a

commentary of the lesson and to record conversations as well as a ready reckoner of graded criteria to tick.

Hence it makes sense to remove some of the fear of the whole process and engage staff in designing the paperwork. Not only will they get a whole lot of CPD in the process, but there is something comforting about knowing the rules of the game before you start playing.

3. Focus on just one thing

If you want to be really lazy, yet still have an opportunity to improve a colleague's teaching, then agree to focus on just one thing for either just part or the whole of the lesson. And stick to it. A rising tide lifts all ships. Likewise with the many different components of teaching. In my experience, focusing on just one aspect serves to help other issues as well. And by agreeing to give and receive feedback solely on that one aspect, and making the process relatively simple and pain free, you may well have broken down the barrier to them volunteering for their own Lazy Lesson observation.

4. Everyone's an inspector

With all the many benefits for observing lessons properly being so clear, why should the responsibility for the process fall solely on a small team of, often the most senior, staff? The more observers the better in my book. And the more observers, the more observations. Everyone wins. So, develop lesson observations in what will ultimately be a Lazy Way by training colleagues and making it a requirement that they too observe lessons. If you are worried about the validity of the final grade that is given, ask yourself what training you have had and then arrange for your colleagues to have the same. For, without wishing to discredit our Ofsted inspectors, it might not take as long as you think to train someone in the art of observation. And remember, you will have had a head start, as you are still in the classroom delivering the very things you are meant to be looking out for.

5. Observer-free observations

You may be worried that colleagues will fully embrace the Lazy Observation of Learning and, as a result of an onslaught of lesson observations, you will have a cover nightmare. Well, as nightmares go it is probably one that (a) you did not predict under the current system of observations and (b) you might just need to manage because as with all nightmares it will be quickly over and the status quo returned (which may mean the nightmare has continued – in every sense).

But if you still need help then employ some cover-free observers, aka video cameras. Filming lessons using a fish-eye lens and microphone so you can capture the visuals and sound from the whole classroom is a wonderful (albeit initially scary) way of developing your staff through what you can describe, with appropriate technological cool, on your school development plan as 'e-observations'. To develop it into a CPD activity (and not just sixty minutes of you cringing) you could share the footage of the lesson with a colleague and ask them to tag a commentary to the lesson. You can then meet up to compare notes.

You could also edit the film into snippets that form clips of best practice (or howling professional blunders – you choose!) to be shared as a training resource for the whole staff, thus making a 'Khan Academy' of professional development. Bearing in mind that a suggestion which begins 'You could ...' is not always in the Lazy teacher's best interests, to stay true to the Lazy Way get students to edit the film, looking for effective behaviours for learning that take place in the lesson and what they and the teachers do to promote and sustain them. After all, it is as much, if not more, about them as it is about you. They have conditions of service as well.

It is said it takes two to tango and the same is true of the observation process. But if you have an observer who won't tango, you can still go through the process yourself in every lesson. And once a few lessons have passed during which you have had no one to have a conversation with, you might even start to feel disappointed. Take that as a really good sign that you are looking forward to your next observation and that the culture of lesson observations in your school is rapidly changing.

Chapter 5

INSTITUTIONALISING PROGRESS - IN A LAZY WAY

Chapter 5
Institutionalising Progress – In a Lazy Way

I don't know about you, but some of my best ideas come to me when I'm feeling bored, angry, mischievous or, if I'm in a meeting, sometimes all three. When feeling like this I tend to turn my ire towards aspects of the educational system that might actually be undoing student progress at the same time as we try to create it (is it no wonder we are exhausted at the end of a term playing a one-man game of tug of war with ourselves?). And in highlighting these aspects, you start to ask those awkward questions about how it could be done differently so that it *did* make a genuine difference to what we are here to do.

Awkward questions around what we do might include:

- Why is learning so different between Year 6 and Year 7?

- Why are lessons the length they are?

- Why do we teach the subjects we do?

- Why do we celebrate collapsed curriculum days as beacons of learning but then revert back to what, by definition, is not a beacon of learning?

- Why do we report in the way we do? Is there not enough feedback happening on a daily basis? Why do we write a special 'report'?

- Why is the year divided up as it is?

- Do other professions close for five days a year of training?

- Why does the heating go on and off on set days of the year?

■ Why can't I choose who I see on parents' evenings?

■ Who is the staffroom milk snatcher?

OK, not so much the last one as I am lucky enough to be in a staffroom where tea, coffee and milk are provided. The only downside is the fun has gone from stealing a little drop of milk from someone's container and then re-marking the pen mark on the side, which the owner had used as some sort of security device, a few millimetres lower to equate for the fact that some milk was missing. Little did the rightful owner know that my new level mark meant that their sense of satisfaction that their security device had seen off the milk snatcher was woefully misplaced! And so you do not get the wrong impression, I did randomly place a pint of milk in the fridge to offset my guilt. After I was caught. Pen in hand.

Still, the other questions are ones that are perhaps not easily solved. And if they are easily answered, and you are being honest, the answers may not always have much to do with learning.

The impulse to change some aspects of our educational processes in schools to support progress is not born out of some macho desire to bend people to my will, to spread innovation for innovation's sake or to make my mark, but because the job is hard enough as it is, without one arm tied behind your back. In addition, many responses to the awkward questions fail to mention an important word – learning. 'We can't do that because it would have a negative effect on student learning' is a counter-argument I can live with. At least it is the starting point for a professional conversation that has the right element at its core. 'We can't do it!' masquerading as 'We won't do it!' is a different matter altogether.

What's more, there is little point in focusing on progress in our lessons if it is being undone by the systems all around us. Whilst at times we might like to see our classrooms as little oases, it is far better to have a whole school focused on progress with supplementary systems that also support that goal.

It is our job to ensure these systems support and enhance learning and create the best possible culture in which learners can progress, regardless of their pace, their starting point or their final destination. This also entails redesigning systems so they eliminate the hours wasted on administration and time spent in meetings that don't make anything better but keeps everybody busy. Time not spent in meetings is time we can all spend focusing on learning.

I don't put forward this view as some sort of work-to-rule militant. Far from it. Of course there are meetings we actually need to attend and admin is up there amongst the necessary evils along with death, taxes and penalty shoot-outs. What I'm cautious about, is that, in the same way that we sometimes find ourselves teaching in the manner we were taught, we just might end up leading a school by the same systems by which we were led when we were further down the heap. Someone needs to know how to break the cycle. After all, we want to institutionalise laziness, not inefficiency.

To assess to what extent the cycle needs to be broken in your school, simply try this evaluative statement and see how many systems (or parts of lessons) fail the test:

Does this process enhance learning in order to maximise the chances of student progress?

Many will fail. They certainly did when we started putting systems to the test in our school. Whilst every school needs routines and systems, you need to ensure that they all focus on helping you achieve progress with learning. There are already enough factors working against progress without us designing systems to add to the list.

This chapter explores three areas of school life where, if you follow the principle of 'letting learning lead' as opposed to 'trying to lead learning', you will increase the potential for progress – in all its forms. All in exchange for a few twists and tweaks born out of letting your boredom, anger and sense of mischief ask the odd awkward question. Maybe there is a point to meetings after all.

The Lazy Way to lead meetings and make progress

For the most part, schools are neatly divided up into year terms, key stages, houses, subjects, faculties or even whole-school learning themes. Each area will have a leader, possibly a deputy as well, who will always attend a pre-programmed series of meetings on set evenings throughout the year. Normally it involves those with responsibility points coming together so information can begin its long free-fall from 'on high' through the hierarchy to the classroom teacher at the chalkface (and from there, who knows ...).

Now, whilst this may paint a stereotypical picture, it is by far the most common approach in schools. But what if we were brave and proposed a few twists and tweaks to the status quo and challenged the structure, content and timing? If we wanted more progress in the classroom we would do something different. It's the same with meetings.

1. **Always start with learning and leave the admin until last**

    Like lessons and James Bond films starring Daniel Craig, people are more engaged at the start and end of meetings than the middle. So take advantage of higher energy levels at the start and talk learning first and foremost. Then take advantage of the 'final straight' energy and people's desire to get out of the door at the end to talk about all things administrative. Just see how the room comes alive when someone utters, 'Any other business?' People trip over themselves to say, 'No', and agree the date of the next meeting without so much as looking at their diaries if it means they get out the door quicker. So it is a perfect time to get agreement on some issue or for someone to quickly fill in the tick list of exam entries. What's more, anything that isn't either about learning or the smooth running of the school can go without guilt into the wasteland that is the middle of the meeting, never to be heard of again. The school policy on differentiating a trainer from a shoe is my favourite, followed by whether it is appropriate to distinguish length of skirt as 'just above the knee' as this might be femur-ist. Please!

We think carefully how we structure our lessons to maximise learning and make the most of students' time. A meeting, its agenda and participants are no different. Just think of all the classroom ideas you could deploy in a meeting! Progress Paparazzi anyone?

2. Every meeting a learning meeting

Always model the same sorts of discussion and thinking skills with colleagues that you expect to see in the classroom. If it's good enough to engage learners, then it's good enough to engage attendees at a meeting. What's the difference? So start the meeting with a strategy to refocus and align everyone ready for the agenda ahead. I know of quite a few schools which start a meeting with one of Ian Gilbert's Thunks™, a question with no right or wrong answer that really gets the creative, divergent thinking juices flowing.

You could also have a team rota for who will present new ideas that are working for them as a standing item on the agenda based on learning. The rota is important so the weight of responsibility does not fall on the 'T+L keener' whose ideas are easily dismissed with a 'Yeah, tried that. Didn't work'. Regardless of whether you have been teaching for two months or twenty years, each and every class will be different, meaning you are always developing new approaches. Or you should be.

Also agree when you are going to witness each other actually *using* these ideas in the classroom. It is easy to nod in agreement as you sit around the table before retreating to your classroom and closing the door for the next fortnight.

We check progress with students to maximise learning. Engineer the same atmosphere with colleagues. It is part of our commitment to role modelling great learning (and avoiding hypocrisy).

3. **Every meeting celebrates progress**

    And not just of the students. Always, always, always make sure you find any opportunity to celebrate the success and progress of the team in the meeting. It changes mindsets and makes people feel great – which is not an altogether bad state to be in at a meeting. Especially when you know what is coming up!

    Compare that with how many colleagues arrive at meetings mentally rehearsing how many to-do lists they will come away with this time and planning how they will fill the meeting time with their own personal progression, as opposed to the team's, and undertake some discreet diary or planner filling so as to save five minutes later (or not to fall asleep).

    A simple bit of public – and sometimes private – praise about the difference we are making ensures the job feels all the more worthwhile. It is why we came into the profession – to make a difference (and not to sit in meetings visualising the crossword or working out what we are teaching tomorrow).

4. **Time of meetings**

    It's 3.40 p.m. It's the second Tuesday of term. It must be subject/year team/house meetings (delete as applicable). You can always see people after the summer holiday writing in a year's worth of meeting dates in their freshly printed planners. Whilst we need some organisational structure to help people plan busy lives, is a meeting held at the end of a full day's work and on a predetermined date fixed months in advance the best way to go about it? (Clue – the answer is no!)

Deliberately sounding like a broken record, let me take you back to the notion of putting learning at the heart of every-thing, of letting the learning lead and not leading the learning. Experience from the lazy learning classroom says we could seriously benefit from a more flexible approach to meetings in our schools. For example, when we offer choice about what order the learning comes in or when the learning takes place within the overall lesson framework we have set out, we max-imise engagement. So why not with meetings?

What would happen if you decided when you should meet based on criteria that were all around improving learning? Linked to this, why not suggest that individual teams fix the dates of meetings? Meetings that are designed around improv-ing learning outcomes for your students may mean you get longer meetings (ones that go on until you agree, as opposed to ones where you agree so they don't go on) but you will also end up with fewer of them. A great lazy result.

In one school I heard of, a team swapped their after-school meetings – those held when they were, I think the medical term is, knackered, not to mention the childcare commitments they had – to one Saturday morning per term.

Another model that is becoming popular is to hold short pre-school meetings (which is effectively formalising, and thereby quite rightly recognising, what happens anyway). It is an approach that can be highly effective in institutionalising changes to the learning ethos in your school, setting people up for the day ahead and clarifying just what impact you want to have on learning.

Of course, you can still have dates when maybe the whole school can come together. But the offer of allowing teams to choose when they meet models trust, respect and professional-ism – something which is key amongst the staff of any school.

5. Who attends meetings?

Getting the right people doing the right job is crucial to progress in a school. Getting the right students completing the right task is crucial to progress in the lesson. As is getting the right student in the right group for group work. Many a technique is deployed by teachers to make sure Ricky and Robbie don't end up sitting in the same group together because, well, we all know what does and doesn't happen when they do ('mucking about' and 'learning' respectively).

The same is true of meetings. And with meetings costing hundreds of pounds per hour in staff salaries, having the right people around the table is crucial. If a particular individual is genuinely not needed at a certain meeting, then simply let them get on with something else, something that will improve learning. There should be no hard feelings on either side, quite the opposite.

To ensure you do end up with the right people around the right table at the right time, why not use some sort of meeting delegate checklist, a process designed to maximise the progress in every meeting:

- Have you got representatives from all the areas affected by the items on the agenda, people who are best qualified to contribute? Remember, simply being called 'Head of ...' or 'Leader of ...' does not necessarily mean that is the best person, at least not for every meeting.

- Is there someone looking for professional development opportunities who would benefit more from the meeting than those who are there, or who should at least shadow someone at the meeting?

- Are delegates totally focused on the meeting? If they have a prior school commitment, such as the last dress rehearsal of the school play which has taken twelve months to come together and is currently the *raison d'être* of their being, then probably not. If you find you can't, as it were, assemble an all-star cast for your meeting then, to carry on the drama theme, maybe you should move *your* production.

With this checklist in place you can then use the maxim beloved of all the most discerning nightclub bouncers: 'If your name's not on the list, you're not coming in.'

And whilst you ponder these ideas, remember: no one will be upset about being given the chance not to attend a meeting. They can be prepping their learning presentation for the next one instead.

Performance management – progress management

There is a simple little evidence-gathering technique that you can use to evaluate a school system or routine that I find very power-ful. In keeping with the Lazy Way it is, as you would expect, quick, easy, takes little preparation and consists of one question while eliciting many valuable and game-changing responses. All you have to do is to get a colleague to complete a particular sen-tence. That's it. For example, if you were conducting a review of performance management the sentence could be:

Performance management is ...

You'll be amazed at what comes back at you and how it reveals a whole wealth of understandings (and misunderstandings) about a particular term – information that you can then use to form and inform your subsequent conversations with your colleagues.

Like it? Simple isn't it? Let's try another one. How about starting the process of evaluating the way your school assesses and reports on students' progress:

Our school reporting system is ...

Or how about:

The structure of our school day is ...
Our current policy on homework is ...
Student behaviour is ...
The policy on mobile phones is ...

Now, whilst it may not return a statistical, quantifiable, league table-making, pie chart-producing, crunchable set of data, it does begin to give you an insight into how people feel. And for a process like performance management, and many others in school, how people feel is the basic factor in whether or not it will work, no matter what they tell you. Your job is to marry people's personal feelings and learning for them to become one. Just like in the classroom.

Once you have your qualitative responses about the nature of performance management you can set about improving your school's policy and further strengthening the process of institutionalising the Lazy Way. In fact, you could call it Lazy Leadership (now there's an idea for a book ...).

The following strategies to improve performance management, in your school are all aimed at freeing up teachers to do what they do best: generate progress in the learning of the young people they teach. They are based on real-life practice I have developed through my work with schools up and down the country. In other words, they are all successfully working somewhere. Useful to know next time someone protests with, 'We can't do it like that' or 'That wouldn't work' or 'Have you been at the gin again, Mr Smith?'

Lazy performance management that generates progress

1. Rebrand it

In some schools the system of performance management has become so devalued, discredited and outright toxic that maybe it needs a new name and a fresh start. Like Sellafield. Or the MK Dons. Or the Department for Education. So, avoid a phrase that sends a shiver down the spine of your most hardened colleagues, especially if it comes with Ofsted connotations, and choose something uplifting and engaging (and hopefully not so corny that it ends up being derided on Twitter, unless you use it in a postmodern ironic way). How about Talent Management, Professional Review, Progress Performance, Personal Coaching Targets or something that captures the ethos of your school? Much better than a phrase that instantly generates a sigh, a shiver or a snigger.

2. Never shy away from standards

Setting the targets during a performance management meeting can often take one of two extremes. There are those who couldn't care less and who put down anything simply to speed up the whole process because that once-a-year meeting in which you are trapped with your line manager is still once too often. Or, at the other end of the scale, the specific nature of the targets set, and the CPD needed to achieve it, mean that the member of staff is unlikely to be in school for anything more than four weeks as they research global comparisons in the delivery of long division amongst C1 and C2 white boys

within the Key Stage 2 curriculum. In the field. Flights and hotels included.

But there is a solution. Instead, why not combine the Department for Education's *Teachers' Standards* with your own school development plan in such a way that it will help identify clearly what everyone should be doing? That way we end up with a system that actually rewards us for doing what we should be doing anyway. Imagine then, if you will, a set of performance management targets that read:

■ **Target 1: Undertake role as outlined by Teachers' Standards**

The Teachers' Standards cut through any ambiguity as to what we should be doing and serve as a reminder of the high expectations the profession now has of the Core Teacher, let alone those aspiring to be a Master Teacher. This target covers everything from progress in the performance of students to designing new schemes of learning and keeping up-to-date with professional research and pedagogy.

Similarly, hold leaders to account with standards on leadership. And if you don't want to be (or have to be) beholden to central government, design your own standards for staff. We spend enough time doing it for the students; it is about time we focused on ourselves.

In a blunt summary, Target 1 (although you could question if 'target' is the right word) is doing the job you are paid to do – which must be every head teacher's dream morning briefing: 'Morning everyone, hope you had a nice weekend. Simple message for the week ahead, let's all do the job we are paid to do!'

■ **Target 2: Attend training or action research groups as a delegate or expert (session leader) as a result of lesson observation feedback**

Progress is most likely to occur when school systems interact so that one strand can benefit from another, thus avoiding the need for repetition or paperwork (or at least pointless paperwork). On the documents used for lesson observation feedback, instead of just recording strengths and weaknesses, feed that into performance management and organise training sessions that reflect the weaknesses – and the strengths – of the whole staff. Run by the staff for the staff, these sessions interspersed throughout the year should provide a perfect opportunity to improve the quality of learning in the classroom. They will also enable your 'experts' to develop as leaders as well as offering some of them the, ahem, opportunity to fulfil their 'upper pay scale' commitment to supporting others.

As an alternative to being in a CPD delivery group, other staff could engage in action research groups. Being aware of the most up-to-date in current thinking (and of when it becomes last year's trend) is crucial in our quickly changing profession, especially when coupled with exactly how the new ideas translate into improvements in the classroom. Action research groups can feed back teaching and learning ideas via INSET days, staff meetings, staffroom learning walls and the like, and even through the school newsletter (thus nimbly demonstrating that you value learning for everyone, not just the students). You could even try to get a column in the local newspaper, like some schools have done.

■ **Target 3: Develop and use resources within your team on ... (insert point from school improvement plan here)**

As a result of a school's own self-evaluation or inspection visit the school will have some clear ideas on what improvements to make in the areas of teaching and learning. By every evaluative measure, it makes sense to have everyone working on those particular aspects so you can clearly show improvements across the whole school – changes that will benefit all students. Why, then, have lots of different, uncoordinated and uncontrollable requests for training with patchy improvement in a key area and staff unclear about priorities when there is an opportunity to all work together for the benefit of learning?

■ **Target 4: This time it's personal**

Some staff may choose a fourth target to reflect their own personal interests in a particular area of learning, or an element of the development plan, as agreed with their line manager. It is likely that this will involve leading an action research group or a CPD session. This work will be presented to colleagues – not to mention the governing body – during the course of the year. Alternatively staff may choose an additional target to reflect their career development. Anyway, why wouldn't you want staff who are keen for promotion?

If we recognise that choice engages learners in the classroom, then by applying what we know about learning to performance management this flexible fourth target is a real must. It is the opportunity for those staff who consider the first three targets as simply 'doing the day job' (as some will and good on 'em) to think about their own interests and career development without causing a total administrative and financial headache ensuing from what could have been hundreds of different targets.

When you have a whole class of students working with you, the feeling of rapid progress is obvious. Likewise with your staff. Buy people into some common targets and feel the simplicity that performance management can bring. Assuming you are still calling it that, of course.

---

3.   If the targets are simple then so is the paperwork

Once you agree the common target approach, you can have a very simple approach to paperwork. Pre-printed pro formas are all but complete, containing data on targets, CPD opportunities and methods of how evidence will be collected and presented. It virtually becomes a 'tick box' activity – but one with significant meaning. The time gained from the reduction in paperwork can be re-invested into conversations with the staff about issues such as how they feel about their work, what it is they might be able to offer the school and so on.

4.   Use performance management to spot and capture the hidden skills and talents of the staff and not just measure what you see

What skills and talents are your students/parents/carers/staff hiding under their respective bushels about which you know absolutely nothing? It is surprising what skills people never offer or leave at home simply because no one has ever asked the question: 'What skills and talents have you got that we have never asked you to use in school?'

Just as with the students, we only ever expect to use certain skills when engaged with certain subjects or staff. So you might have amazing musicians outside of your music staff who could contribute to school plays but currently feel they can't as it is the music teacher's/department's role. Or you might have someone with a hidden passion for classic cartoons such as *Tom and Jerry* who would run a lunchtime club for those who might not want to tear around the playground impersonating Wayne Rooney. Or even an amazing cake maker who has never baked a thing in school yet could quite happily be involved in a catering team to raise money at school events. The bigger your staff, the more talent goes untapped. And it is the same for the students. What skills and talents do they leave at home? You just might be surprised.

And the funny thing is that when it is a skill, hobby or talent, it never feels like extra work if you bring it into school on the odd occasion. It's not as if someone will suddenly put you down to teach 200 students music next year. Honest … ish!

5. How do I love thee? Let me count the ways

Do everything that you can to admire your colleagues in lots of lessons and in lots of different ways. Some performance management systems link a single, nominated lesson to the performance management process, which is the same as staking your professional reputation and life savings on the favourite in the 2.30 from Kempton Park. Leave that sort of nerve-inducing, eggs-in-a-single-basket gamble to when the inspection team call. Where you have control and choice, set up a system which gathers evidence on the teaching in your school from a myriad of sources, including observations, feedback from students, parents, colleagues, any outside agencies you may work with and, of course, the individual teacher's personal professional reflections on their year.

By letting learning lead and being progress focused there is a clear rationale for the new performance management process. Or whatever you are going to call it. With that achieved, a next step could be to call together a group of staff and present the ideas outlined above. Follow that up by asking them to imagine you were actually going to implement them, all of them. Then enjoy the process of discussion before seeking clarification and then a creative person-alisation of the ideas to make a hybrid that is just right for your school before asking:

'Under the new system, performance management is ...'

And when they do answer, you may well have just found the staff to present the new performance management policy to their col-leagues. How lazy is that?

And if you are really being lazy, then you will instantly be transfer-ring the whole process into the classroom. Students launching the whole process to their peers, collaboratively agreeing what it is that needs to happen, developing a process of accountability to you and their peers and celebrating the outcomes – which we know will have a common theme of progress. Simple really. Especially when you let learning lead.

Continuing professional self–development (CPsD)

OK, so adding letters to various educational acronyms is somewhat of an inevitability in our job, what with policy update after policy update. Take PSE. Or was it PSHE? Or PSCHE? (You know, the sex and drugs and rock 'n' roll one where you take three of the most alluring and important topics for young people and make worksheets out of them to switch them off all three in the class-room, but very much switch them on in various other rooms.) But please allow this acronym-twist through as an exception before there is a complete embargo. After all, it is good for learning, I assure you. And it gives a whole new lazy slant to the term 'pro-fessional development' – meaning your colleagues will progress without you doing anything!

In its current form, many schools look to develop their workforce and improve their skill set through a variety of innovative and effective – and neither of the aforementioned – approaches. High profile INSET days, teaching and learning residential conferences, external trainers, collaborative twilight sessions, in-house peer-to-peer support sessions ... the list goes on. The onus, though, is on schools developing their staff.

But what expectations does a school have that the workforce develops itself too? What if instead of having just a single continuing professional development (CPD) coordinator, everyone became their own CPsD coordinator? Whilst it might mean a marked change and cultural shift, the potential for your workforce to improve quicker and further suddenly becomes enormous. Be clear that the shift does not mean you are abandoning any school-led professional development. Far from it. But you are highlighting an expectation that, in line with professional standards, staff should be taking a professional responsibility in keeping themselves up-to-date with pedagogical advances.

The benefits of CPsD are huge. Yet, in keeping with our Lazy Leadership principles and wanting progress from everyone, you haven't had to do a thing, other than remind colleagues that professional development is an all year round process, not just for INSET days and holidays. With that mind, what follows is a range of ideas to take professional development away from the isolation of its INSET day home, out of the hands of school leaders, and into the hands of the teachers themselves.

Five ways to achieve CPsD throughout the year

1. Change existing structures to encourage CPsD

Use as many other school structures and routines as possible to support CPsD. For example, tie it in with lesson observation feedback and then link it to CPsD targets or use it during performance management to formalise the use of CPsD.

2. Stars in your eyes

'Today, Matthew, I am going to teach ...' and in you dig to the 'Timetable Lucky Dip' to discover your new timetable for the day! In preparation for this moment you need to advertise your annual 'class swap day' a few days in advance, not to encourage staff absence on the day itself but so that nothing is planned that necessitates a specialist teacher in a particular lesson. Then, on the agreed morning, place all the staff time-tables in a lucky dip, gather your colleagues together, switch on the dry ice and let the fun commence!

As well as being a very enjoyable experience, it also gets us right back to the basics of learning because suddenly you are stripped of your subject knowledge or usual age range experience and you have to rely on sheer gumption; it also helps you know what it feels like for those children struggling in a particular class. It is fascinating how people respond to such a challenge, and to observe the approaches they take. For these reasons it is a crucial part of such a learning experience that you meet at the end of the day to debrief, share reflections on what has been learnt and explore not only what the school has learnt but also how teachers will take forward what they have learnt from the experience when normality returns and they retreat to the safety of their own classroom, classes and subject areas once again.

3.   Showcases and learning drop-ins

This is the CPsD equivalent of a mash-up between the part of Noel Edmonds's *Swap Shop* where Cheggers would swap an Action Man tank for a Big Foot, or the like, a Blue Peter bring-and-buy sale and Freecycle. Although, having said that, there will be some of you reading this who are too young to know who Cheggers is or what *Swap Shop* was but others who are too old to know what a mash-up is. Sigh!

Basically, I am referring to a giant guide to CPsD in action where you can swap your ideas for new ideas. What you do is create a great big board in the staffroom that is divided into two. On one side you write 'What I am offering' and on the other side 'What I would like'. You then give each member of staff two giant sticky notes or cut-out coloured stars which they fill in and place on the display, putting one in each column.

It is a very simple way of keeping momentum for CPsD going throughout the year. If you want to, you could start adding feedback onto the sticky notes as to what went well, what happened when you tried it with your group, funny comments and, of course, the all important impact on progress in the lesson. You might even have a tally system or stars to acknowledge how many people have dropped in because if the learning activity is proving popular, it may be time to ask others to model it.

And if it is a learning activity that is helping all learners to progress significantly whenever and wherever it is used, maybe it is time to tell *all* staff about it. This is something you could do through a ten-minute 'staff learning meeting' which you hold in lieu of the same old morning briefing. Imagine the impact this could have compared with the same old announcements, dished out and then forgotten by the time you get to your classroom in time-honoured fashion. The only rules connected with the ideas board is that everyone must offer and request something and everyone must see at least five people over the course of the year. This is, after all, CPsD.

4. **On-line CPsD**

By letting learning lead, we can once again draw on what is happening in the classroom and look at how technology might support CPsD. The emergence of Twitter, blogging, chatrooms and on-line video resources have really made CPsD a viable and free, yet high quality, proposition.

For on-line learning to have its maximum impact in developing CPsD, you may well have to show some direct leadership. Do not get confused: I am not suggesting you run a session. But it could be worthwhile setting up your students as digital leaders in your school not only so they can train the staff on the benefits of on-line learning, or even simply how to go about it, but also by being the sort of school that teaches and learns from each other.

Accepting, as we do with a class, that not everyone is massively turned on by computers and subsequently may not be stimulated by having a Twitter account or hanging out in a chatroom with a load of strangers (when they could be down the pub), offer colleagues the opportunity to take ownership of the CPsD library instead; that is to say a physical library with books, real ones, with paper and everything. The stimulus from the leadership may be splashing out on a few titles (I can think of two I would recommend!) or subscribing to some educational journals that actually help teachers teach better. After that you could offer partial subsidies on books that are requested or full subsidies on books that then lead to a staff CPsD session.

Just imagine if a book club sprang up in your staffroom. If it's good enough for Oprah and Richard and Judy, it's good enough for you. Colleagues chatting and debating teaching and learning and wanting to progress in their own free time?

Now there's some genuine proof of the benefits of Lazy Leadership when it comes to staff development.

5. Sharing CPsD with others outside your school

I am lucky enough in my role to visit many schools during the year whilst also having a base at my own school where I am a real teacher, as well as a real member of a real leadership team (although surreal might describe it better when we indulge in the activities I am describing here). As a result of this I can personally vouch for the energising and uplifting effect of spending time with colleagues from other schools, not only in person but also on-line.

One such example of face-to-face sharing of ideas is the concept of TeachMeets. These informal conferences are springing up all over the country. In their simplest form they are best described as an informal twilight/evening session where people involved in education can come together to present ideas in short snappy time slots (like a TEDx for those people too lazy to organise a TEDx). They are fun, well attended, often have great hospitality and – and this is the killer app – they are totally free. What's more, you walk away with a whole load of ideas – guaranteed. So why not host one or put on a minibus to take staff to your nearest one? You can find out where your nearest one is by searching for TeachMeet on the internet.

Whilst some schools produce a teaching and learning newsletter, few do it as a collaboration between a cluster of schools, but why not? It is another great way of promoting CPsD all year long. What works especially well is if you combine schools with different Key Stages, as there is so much we can learn from each other. The problem with newsletters is that they often rely on the same few people to come up with another five whizzy ideas (who incidentally will probably be the people already engaged in being the very best they can and making progress along with the students). To combat this, make sure you promote the expectation that everyone in the school should and will contribute by having a pre-published rota of who is contributing what and when.

The newsletter can be produced in both paper and on-line form. Using tools such as www.issuu.com you could also link it to your website, tweet about it or, if you are really old-fashioned, email it to the other schools who contributed, wherever they may be in the world.

Progress the Lazy Way – an Epilogue

At any point in time there will be a drive for educational change and improvement. This is magnified with the emergence of any new league table that puts the UK below Country Y and now, rather worryingly for the politicians, below Country X. (I can't reveal the countries for fear of someone quoting this as a fact and introducing yet another national obsession into someone else's education system. Having Finland fulfil that role is already enough.)

This is not to suggest change is not needed in our profession. It is. In many ways the profession needs to follow its own advice and become less 'do as I say' and more 'do as I do'. We are all too quick to offer advice to the students: 'You need to be able to learn in different ways so you do not become illiterate in the twenty-first century' or 'You need to be able learn so you are fully prepared for careers that may not even exist yet' (even if it is the same advice that has been applicable for the last few hundred years).

But how do we face up to the same challenges in our own profession? We now have more understanding, more research and data and greater pedagogical understanding of learning than ever before. Perhaps too much. Is it hands up or hands down? Group work or individual work? Shouting out or whispering quietly? Rows of tables or clusters of tables? Knowledge or skills? Chaucer or comics? How do we ever get a consensus when debate and academic evidence can be used to prove most things in a classroom?

However, like the lettering through a stick of rock, there is one thing that will remain constant throughout and is unequivocally guaranteed to be the same in any classroom anywhere: the need for progress.

There is a moral and professional responsibility that this should happen. And whilst we can debate the merits of an education inspection system and any government initiatives, the reality is

that our job is an incredibly personal one. It is a job built upon a respectful rapport between ourselves and our students.

What greater way to show the students respect for learning than by putting them at the centre and making them the focus of the learning? And when you do that, the students are well on the way to getting what they deserve – their progress comes before your performance. After all, who is the laziest one in the class?

Recommended On-line Resources

http://learningspy.co.uk

http://museumbox.e2bn.org/index.php

www.cueprompter.com

www.howbigreally.com

www.reallusion.com

www.voki.com

www.techsmith.com

www.khanacademy.org

www.issuu.com

www.ictevangelist.com

www.thunks.co.uk

Bibliography

Department for Education, *Teachers' Standards in England from September 2012*. Available at http://media.education.gov.uk/assets/files/pdf/t/teachers%20standards%20from%20september%202012.pdf (accessed 24 April 2012).

Friedman, T., *The World is Flat: The Globalized World in the Twenty-First Century*. London: Penguin, 2005.

Gilbert, I., *The Little Book of Thunks: 260 Questions to Make Your Brain Go Ouch!* Carmarthen, Wales: Crown House Publishing, 2007.

Gilbert, I., *Why Do I Need A Teacher When I've Got Google?* Abingdon: Routledge, 2011.

Ofsted, *The Framework for School Inspection from January 2012*. Ref: 090019. Available at http://www.ofsted.gov.uk/resources/framework-for-school-inspection-january-2012 (accessed 24 April 2012).

Smith, J., *The Lazy Teacher's Handbook: How Your Students Learn More When You Teach Less*. Carmarthen, Wales: Crown House Publishing, 2010.

Bringing together some of the most innovative practitioners working in education today. www.independentthinkingpress.com

The Big Book of Independent Thinking: Do things no one does or do things everyone does in a way no one does — Edited by Ian Gilbert
ISBN 978-190442438-3

Little Owl's Book of Thinking: An Introduction to Thinking Skills — Ian Gilbert
ISBN 978-190442435-2

The Little Book of Thunks: 260 questions to make your brain go ouch! — Ian Gilbert
ISBN 978-184590062-5

The Buzz: A practical confidence builder for teenagers — David Hodgson
ISBN 978-190442481-9

Are You Dropping the Baton?: How schools can work together to get transition right — Dave Harris Edited by Ian Gilbert
ISBN 978-184590081-6

Leadership with a Moral Purpose: Turning Your School Inside Out — Will Ryan Edited by Ian Gilbert
ISBN 978-184590084-7

The Little Book of Big Stuff about the Brain — Andrew Curran Edited by Ian Gilbert
ISBN 978-184590085-4

Rocket Up Your Class!: 101 high impact activities to start, end and break up lessons — Dave Keeling Edited by Ian Gilbert
ISBN 978-184590134-9

The Lazy Teacher's Handbook: How Your Students Learn More When You Teach Less — Jim Smith Edited by Ian Gilbert
ISBN 978-184590289-6

The Learner's Toolkit: Developing Emotional Intelligence, Instilling Values for Life, Creating Independent Learners and Supporting the SEAL Framework for Secondary Schools — Jackie Beere Edited by Ian Gilbert
ISBN 978-184590070-0

www.independentthinkingpress.com

Bringing together some of the most innovative practitioners working in education today. www.independentthinkingpress.com

The Little Book of Charisma: Applying the Art and Science — David Hodgson Edited by Ian Gilbert
ISBN 978-184590293-3

The Little Book of Inspirational Teaching Activities: Bringing NLP into the Classroom — David Hodgson Edited by Ian Gilbert
ISBN 978-184590136-3

The Little Book of Music for the Classroom: Using Music to Improve Memory, Motivation, Learning and Creativity — Nina Jackson Edited by Ian Gilbert
ISBN 978-184590091-5

The Little Book of Values: Educating children to become thinking, responsible and caring citizens — Julie Duckworth Edited by Ian Gilbert
ISBN 978-184590135-6

The Primary Learner's Toolkit — Jackie Beere Edited by Ian Gilbert
ISBN 978-184590395-4

The Perfect (Ofsted) Lesson — Jackie Beere Edited by Ian Gilbert
ISBN: 978-184590460-9

Young, Gifted and Bored — David George Edited by Ian Gilbert
ISBN: 978-184590680-1

Inspirational Teachers Inspirational Learners — Will Ryan Edited by Ian Gilbert
ISBN: 978-184590443-2

The Book of Thunks®: Is not going fishing a hobby? and other possibly impossible questions to stretch your brain and annoy your friends — Ian Gilbert
ISBN 978-184590092-2

They Did You Can: How to achieve whatever you want in life with the help of your sporting heroes — Michael Finnigan
ISBN 978-178135004-1

www.independentthinkingpress.com

Bringing together some of the most innovative practitioners working in education today. www.independentthinkingpress.com

The Little Book of Bereavement for Schools — Ian Gilbert
ISBN 978-184590464-7

Dancing About Architecture — Phil Beadle Edited by Ian Gilbert
ISBN: 978-184590725-9

Where will I do my pineapples? — Gill Kelly Edited by Ian Gilbert
ISBN: 978-184590696-2

Oops!: Helping children learn accidentally — Hywel Roberts Edited by Ian Gilbert
ISBN: 978-178135009-6

The Perfect Ofsted Inspection — Jackie Beere Edited by Ian Gilbert
ISBN: 978-178135000-3

Independent Thinking — Ian Gilbert
ISBN 978-178135055-3

Thinking Allowed — Mick Waters
ISBN 978-178135056-0

The Discipline Coach: Powerful, practical strategies for helping your students get the best out of themselves — Jim Roberson Edited by Ian Gilbert
ISBN 978-178135005-8

The Little Book of Awe and Wonder : A Cabinet of Curiosities
— Dr Matthew McFall
ISBN 978-178135001-0

The Philosophy Shop: Ideas, activities and questions to get people, young and old, thinking philosophically — Peter Worley and The Philosophy Foundation
ISBN 978-178135049-2

My School Improvement Doodle Book — Ben Keeling
ISBN 978-1-78135-051-5

The Little Book of Laughter for the Classroom and Staffroom —
Dave Keeling and Stephanie Davies
ISBN 978-178135008-9

www.independentthinkingpress.com

Bringing together some of the most innovative practitioners working in education today. www.independentthinkingpress.com

The Perfect Teacher Coach — Terri Broughton Edited by Jackie Beere
ISBN 978-178135003-4

Perfect Assessment for Learning — Claire Gadsby Edited by Jackie Beere
ISBN 978-178135002-7

The Perfect Ofsted English Lesson — David Didau Edited by Jackie Beere
ISBN 978-178135052-2

Boring, Irrelevant and Hard: How to develop outstanding maths lessons that aren't any of the above — Ian Taylor
ISBN 978-178135050-8

Brave Heads: How to lead your school without selling your soul — Dave Harris Edited by Ian Gilbert
ISBN 978-178135048-5

Trivium 21st Century: Preparing young people for the future with lessons from the past — Martin Robinson Edited by Ian Gilbert
ISBN 978-178135054-6

Full on Learning: Involve me and I'll understand — Zoë Elder Edited by Ian Gilbert
ISBN 978-184590681-8

Altogether Now ... The Ultimate Plenary Book — Phil Beadle
ISBN 978-178135053-9

The Twenty-first Century Assembly Book — Will Ryan
ISBN 978-178135007-2

The Little Book of Dyslexia: Both sides of the classroom — Joe Beech
Edited by Ian Gilbert
ISBN 978-178135010-2

www.independentthinkingpress.com

The Lazy Teacher's Handbook

How Your Students Learn More
When You Teach Less

by Jim Smith

ISBN: 978-184590289-6

Ever wondered what would happen if you stopped teaching in your lessons? You might be surprised. If you want your students to learn more and you to work less, then this book provides you with all the arguments and evidence you need to become a lazy, but outstanding teacher. Gathered over 10 years in the classroom, this handbook of tried-and-tested techniques shifts the emphasis away from the teaching and onto the learning, and makes your life so much easier in the process.

This powerful book is packed full of easy-to-apply and highly effective strategies (which Ofsted have rated as 'outstanding'). What's more, they all have the seal of approval of real students in real classrooms. In fact, many of them have been thought up by the students themselves, but that's why Jim Smith is called the Lazy Teacher. So, next time someone tells you to get a life, this book will make it possible.